CHOOSING AND USING A CONSULTANT

CHOOSING AND USING A CONSULTANT

A Manager's Guide to Consulting Services

HERMAN HOLTZ

JOHN WILEY & SONS
New York • Chichester • Brisbane • Toronto • Singapore

Published by John Wiley & Sons, Inc.

Library of Congress Cataloging in Publication Data:

Holtz, Herman.
Choosing and using a consultant: a manager's guide to consulting services/Herman Holtz.
p. cm.
Bibliography: p.
ISBN 0-471-60287-6
1. Consultants. 2. Consultants—Selection and appointment.
I. Title.
HD69.C6H619 1989 88-31693
658.4′6—dc19 CIP

Printed in the United States of America
10 9 8 7 6 5 4 3 2 1

PREFACE

WHY DO YOU NEED THIS BOOK? WHAT WILL IT DO FOR YOU?

Society long ago defined "the oldest profession," perhaps accurately, perhaps not. It was not the profession of consulting that was so identified, but if consulting is not the oldest profession, it is certainly *among* the oldest. There has been no time in recorded history when consultants have not been in evidence, although the term *consultant* was not necessarily applied to these professionals prior to modern times. Monarchs and other heads of state have always had staffs of ministers and advisors to counsel them. The president of the United States has his cabinet—the secretaries and other officials who head up federal agencies—as well as his White House staff. But even so, he calls in consultants from the private sector to form special presidential commissions and otherwise carry out support missions. The chief executive of every large organization has a staff of subordinate officers as well as outside experts to call upon for counsel.

How do heads of state choose and use their ministers, secretaries, chiefs of staff, and other consultants? Not always by completely rational means, certainly, for there are always political considerations, personal biases, and considerations of expediency. This has always been so, because decisions often must be based on factors other than efficiency and effectiveness. It is simply not always clear what the decisive factors ought to be regarding a decision; there are often concealed problems to baffle and frustrate the executive who seeks the help of experts in some field. The need for outside help grows almost daily.

Consulting has grown steadily over the centuries, both as a profession and as a business. That growth is a natural consequence of society's steady evolution toward greater complexity. It is only partially the effect of burgeoning high technology; it would make itself felt even in the absence of technology as the world population swells, governments topple and are replaced, public officials and government agencies struggle to solve growing social problems, and businesses grow ever more complex. It is an increasingly rare executive or official who can cope with daily problems without the help of specialists of many kinds. Hence the steadily increasing dependence on experts who call themselves *consultants*.

But just what is a consultant? In its narrowest and most restricted definition, a consultant is an expert who is available, for a fee, to render counsel on a problem falling within his or her special field. In its broadest definition, on the other hand, a consultant is any individual or firm (consultants are also companies, in this broad definition) specializing in some field and providing counsel and/or related services in that field for payment.

One more factor: Although many specialist experts tender their services to individuals (e.g., tutoring slow students, helping individuals stop smoking, teaching small-computer technology, etc.), the focus here is principally on the consulting services the average executive needs in order to manage efficiently.

Although I lean toward the broad definition, a consultant, in these pages, is someone who falls between the extremes just described. That is, the term is used in its broadest sense except in discussing certain professional and technical experts who meet the broad definition but are well identified by other generic titles and do not normally consider themselves to be consultants. Even that exception has its own exceptions.

Lawyers, physicians, architects, and a few other classes of

professionals do not normally regard themselves as consultants, and I do not, therefore, include them generally as a class. Yet, they—especially physicians—sometimes do function as consultants; they are called in to consult. Since it is not possible to define the term without a certain amount of ambiguity, so be it.

More important than the question of definition is the question of how to choose and use consultants: how to find and/or select the consultant best suited to your own purposes. Before that question can be answered, however, the question of how (and when) you know that you need to get the help of a consultant must be raised.

This resolves into the following three general problems:

1. Recognizing you have a problem that is beyond your normal scope
2. Analyzing your problem to decide just what kind of help (what kind of consultant) you need
3. Finding, choosing, and using the consultant

Each of these general problems has concealed within it a number of other problems such as the few representative ones listed here:

1. Overcoming reluctance to admit to yourself that you need help in solving a problem
2. Evaluating the costs quoted by applicants
3. Evaluating applicants' credentials
4. Handling the myriad chores required to search out candidates for consulting assignments and to manage them after they have been hired

That is what this book is about. Its major objective is to help you solve all these problems. You will be led through the necessary processes, with full discussions, and gain a set of tools to use on the job.

HERMAN HOLTZ

Silver Spring, Maryland
April 1989

CONTENTS

CHOOSING AND USING A CONSULTANT

Chapter One

Modern Management Dilemmas

Not since the Industrial Revolution has there been such diverse, rapid, and fundamental change in commerce and industry, nor has there ever been such emphasis on and uncertainty about management and its role in the modern business/industrial world. This produces many dilemmas.

A BRIEF OVERVIEW OF MODERN MANAGEMENT CONCERNS

The role of management today is increasingly difficult to perform and even to define. These are times of unprecedentedly rapid technological, political, social, business, and economic change. Much of the change and the problems it creates stem from technological growth, but there are also many other factors. Following are just a few of the major problems facing today's managers.

Unions and automation. Issues concerning unions and automation are linked in many ways. Managers still must deal with the traditional union problems, which are made more serious today by a shrinking union-member base in many industries that adds to the anxieties of union leaders. But questions of automation, especially in industries with high labor costs, arise more and more frequently. This requires managers to weigh the investment costs of automation against its potential savings and to consider how automation will affect relations with the unions. Automation is often a great problem in terms of how it affects relations directly with employees and indirectly through their unions. Certainly, unions rarely endorse automation, because it leads to a reduction in the number of people (i.e., the number of union members) companies employ.

Management and administrative office systems. The labor-intensive systems of the past are under scrutiny today as a result of elevated labor costs and labor shortages. Formerly it was easy to make decisions, because small companies could not afford computerization. Now it is a different matter; small computers are readily available, but training costs are high and it is difficult to find suitable employees. Managers are compelled to ask themselves, Will computerization pay its own way, at least, and does it show the clear prospect of reducing costs in some way? The

Paragraph

① 312 / 80

How to deal with it.

→ I have learn from consultant

What
who
How ...

Before you begin to search you will need to define
you were looking for articles on railway safety the
you will also have to consider all ending of those w
railway, rail ,railways and safe, safety, safer, etc. a
signals or signalling. To allow for all endings of pa

To search **ANTEnet** you use the standard boolean
For example, to search for articles about Railway
following :

rail* and safe* and si

Once you have typed in your keywords click **Sear**
Box giving the number of records found and a list
adjacent checkboxes, to the left of each title, for e
Display.

To add more keywords to your search or to begin
to the search screen.

To download your search results to disk or to ema
display screen. To do this click **Close** then select
sure that you select the **Word Wrap** option.

real question is this: Can I justify a costly changeover? Which is the best decision: to change or to stand by older methods?

Employee relations. The classic employee problem of a few decades past was one of motivation and productivity: how an employer could motivate employees to be more productive. (The assumption was that employee motivation was the key to productivity, a premise not yet clearly established as fact.) However, one of the most pressing modern personnel problems is drug use, and it is growing steadily more serious. It is so serious, in fact, that it has become a major area of address by consultants who furnish employee assistance programs to employers. However, there are many other employee problems today, among them the acute shortages of labor in many areas, the high cost of hospitalization insurance and other fringe benefits, and the intensified focus on and demand for employee retirement programs.

Legal problems. The United States has become a highly litigious society, and this is a major problem for many managers. To at least some degree, the problem has been severely aggravated by federal legislation covering workplace safety and health, product safety, pension plans, and many other employee-related matters. These laws evidently encourage litigation by providing plaintiffs with what they believe to be a substantial basis for their lawsuits. In any case, retaining legal counsel on a continuing basis only addresses the symptoms. The real problem—and the more sensible solution—is prevention, arranging business operations in a way that discourages and prevents lawsuits.

Regulation and control. The same new laws and programs that tend to encourage litigation also cause managers anxiety in other ways. True, these legal requirements reflect social and economic changes that are important to a modern society more concerned with individual rights and justice than past generations were. The proliferation of new laws and regulations is a source of worry for managers who are responsible for assuring compliance with them. That is not the entire problem, however. There is also the problem of increased government control—some would say intrusion—that often makes it far more difficult for managers to carry out their responsibilities while maintaining profitability.

Tax laws. Although they have accountants, often full-fledged comptrollers, looking after fiscal matters, managers cannot be indifferent to the almost annual changes in tax laws. These changes are another of the many management dilemmas managers must surmount in an increasingly complex and government-controlled world.

Physical or plant security. In recent years this has become a serious problem, reflected in a general increase in lawlessness, marked increase in industrial espionage, and the advent of burglary and unlawful entry by computer. All kinds of new security services and devices are now being employed. Infrared and ultrasonic sound are two relatively recent approaches to intrusion-detection mechanisms, but more and more, employers have taken to employing human guard forces on their premises and considering whatever other new measures are offered.

Data and information security. This is even more critical than physical or plant security. In an era of innovation, especially technological innovation, companies increasingly need to safeguard the products and processes they develop. With industrial espionage by competitors and predators—actual spying on and theft of company proprietary data—and purloining by former employees (some of whom are starting their own competitive firms while others are joining the ranks of a competitor's employees), the problem has taken on major proportions. It is further complicated by the fact that much of the confidential and proprietary data, if not all of it, is computer data. Despite the many and various schemes for coding files and controlling access to them, the best of computer-security systems have often been defeated by energetic and resourceful computer pirates.

Industrial decline. In the future the United States will almost surely be far less dependent on its traditional base of heavy industry and more dependent on the newer information industries. Managers of businesses that are still dependent on heavy industry must cope with this decline. (It is, of course, most unlikely that any of the traditional industries will wither and disappear completely, despite a possible decline.) For many managers this means facing the problem of capturing a larger share of the remaining market, while for others it means diversifying into other industries, those that are related to or at least unaffected by the trend away from heavy industries. However, many who have acquired diversified companies have found it far more difficult than they had anticipated to learn to operate them profitably. The acquisition of new and different companies therefore constitutes a dilemma of its own.

Support services. It is becoming increasingly difficult to provide adequate service to customers today, as support services continue to deteriorate. The continually rising costs of many services such as printing, advertising, drafting, and delivery (including mailing and shipping) are only a few of the areas of concern. Today's managers face the constant problem of what can be done to reduce these costs without sacrificing service. Managers must also cope with problems of obsolescence and lack of dependability, since many traditional services have deteriorated steadily in quality and reliability. For example, today's managers cannot be sure that shipments by conventional means will be delivered on a timely basis or even at all. The deterioration of traditional shipping and delivery services, especially in the postal system, has led to a rapid rise in the overnight-delivery industry despite its high cost. Even telephone services have become more expensive since the reorganization and partial breakup of AT&T.

Market competition. The market for most products and services is becoming more and more competitive. Top-level managers, whether or not they are directly responsible for sales, are always ultimately responsible, if only for hiring, directing, and retaining effective marketing and/or sales managers.

Miscellaneous matters. The foregoing was a brief overview of just a few of the many problems and areas of concern to managers today. An even more important question is what it all means in the more global terms of management in general: *What is happening to management?* What is a manager?

THE DILEMMA OF ROLE DEFINITION: WHAT IS A MANAGER?

There are many traditional and conventional definitions of a manager, most of them based on the theory that a manager is best described as someone who gets work done through other people. Of course, that is a definition of the *role* of the manager, and it points up an anomaly: Is the manager a generalist or a specialist?

The reason this is a paradoxical question is that while many believe that management is a science—or perhaps an art—transferred easily from one industry to another, this belief implies that the manager is enough of a generalist to manage all kinds of workers in all kinds of departments and divisions and all kinds of industries. Confounding that idea, however, is the notion that management is itself a specialty that can be applied anywhere with equally good results.

That is the reasoning that led the Apple Computer Company to recruit their current chief executive officer, John Sculley, from Pepsi Cola without considering Sculley's lack of experience in the computer industry to be a handicap in any way. The very diversity of that need to be knowledgeable in a wide variety of areas, many of them of rather recent origin, translates into generalization rather than specialization. Therefore the modern manager is ever more the generalist, striving to be, yet finding it increasingly difficult to be, a qualified specialist in each of dozens of areas. That is another modern management dilemma: Can managers be both specialists and generalists in today's business and industrial world?

The answer lies somewhere between those extremes. It is not possible for any manager, not even a genius, to be a generalist who has expertise in all areas of concern. Yet it is not possible to cope with modern management problems in large organizations—even in government and other non-profit and not-for-profit organizations—without coming to grips with a wide variety of technico-managerial matters. The answer to this basic dilemma will be found in the pages to follow, which are devoted to how managers are coping by using the services of expert specialists known as *consultants*.

Chapter Two

How to Know When You Need a Consultant

Unfortunately, recognition of a need for expert help—or the refusal to recognize such a need—too often has as much subconscious emotional content as rational or objective content.

THE FIRST OF THREE MAJOR PHASES

There are three major phases or factors in choosing a consultant:

1. Deciding that you need a consultant
2. Deciding what kind of consultant you need
3. Choosing the specific consultant best suited to your need

This is the logical sequence; yet these are not strictly sequential events nor are they events that are independent and isolated from one another. They are, in fact, iterative, and although this chapter deals primarily with the first event—how to determine that you need a consultant—it is necessary to discuss other considerations as well. Why this is true will become apparent.

Although this chapter is concerned with determining the need for a consultant, you will find that the three phases are related and cannot be treated in total isolation from one another. For example, it is logically quite difficult to decide whether you need a consultant until you have a good idea of what your need is, based on specific data, and of what kinds of consultants are available and what kinds of services they can provide.

To determine whether you need a consultant, or at least to consider retaining a consultant, you must learn certain facts and rid yourself of commonly held biases and misconceptions. One important observation should be made here: Consulting is not itself a profession; it is a means for practicing a profession, and anyone who provides services on a temporary or project basis is providing a consulting service, whether or not that person bears the title *consultant*.

HOW OBVIOUS IS THE NEED FOR A CONSULTANT?

The question of how to know when and if you need a consultant may appear to be somewhat academic at first glance. That is, you may believe that when you need a consultant that need will be immediately apparent. That may be so in many cases in which the need for a consultant is so obvious as to generate virtually instant and automatic recognition. That is, the manager faced with a complex problem concerning his or her computer is quite likely to say almost immediately upon encountering the problem, "Let's find someone to help us." It is not always true, however. The same manager, faced with a different kind of problem—perhaps writing a manual or designing an inventory system—might react far differently, failing to recognize or at least question doubtfully the need for outside help.

WHY MANY MANAGERS ARE SLOW TO RECOGNIZE THE NEED FOR HELP

Experience in my own field is enlightening in this regard. Among the several services I provide my clients is proposal writing and related services. But it is a relatively rare case when I am called upon at an early stage in the process. That is, clients rarely recognize the need for help early in the proposal-writing process. Distressingly often, they wait until they are in trouble before they acknowledge the need for help from someone with special knowledge and skills.

A common problem is that many people do not regard the ability to write proposals as a specialized skill. Instead, they reason that anyone with an education is fully capable of writing well enough to put together a decent proposal; thus, they often attempt to do so without help and without real knowledge of what is required to do the job well. It is only when much of the allowed time has elapsed—and at best proposal schedules are difficult—that the client begins to recognize that the task is more difficult than it appears and requires special knowledge and skills. At that point the desperate client begins to seek a consultant to help get the proposal written in the few remaining days.

Unfortunately, this type of mistake is all too typical, and it can be costly. One client, late with his report and badgered by his client, the U.S. Army, was given a final deadline as an ultimatum and came pleading for help. He had only two days left to deliver a 750-page report, which existed as a draft but had to be edited, typed, proofed, and printed within 48 hours. It cost him $11,000 to get this done, more than twice what it would have cost had he recognized the need for expert help earlier. Again and again, government agencies pay premiums and penalties to consultants for last-minute rescue efforts when the agencies wait too long to discover that they cannot do the job themselves.

MAKING THE RIGHT DISTINCTIONS

On the other side of the coin, a wise client who was a professional writer called on me for proposal help because he recognized that more than writing skill was involved in writing successful proposals. That is, he perceived that a proposal is a *sales presentation* and the ability to prepare sales material is at least as important to the task as is writing skill. Therefore, I was retained only to help him analyze the request for proposals and suggest a strategy for his proposal, which he was fully capable of writing.

That process involves gaining a good understanding of the client's need (i.e., of the real problem), which is not always readily apparent. In fact, it is not uncommon to find clients describing symptoms when they believe they are describing the problem. (This problem will be discussed in greater detail in the next chapter, but it is necessary to note it now.)

To make the right distinctions, you must try to get a clear view of your need and of what consultants can offer you in the way of services. A good consultant will help you define your problem, but that does not mean that you should not make an effort to do so for yourself first.

WHAT SERVICES DO YOU REALLY NEED?

In deciding whether you need a consultant, you must often think beyond the direct problem. (It may well be that you need consulting help to define or identify the problem before you tackle the job of deciding how you will cope with it.) For example, you may decide that you must have a computer system to modernize and automate your office operations. That is easy enough to say, but there are many questions to answer before you can begin to act. Higher management will want to know how much you need; they will want to look at your budget before they will discuss it seriously. (Higher-level people move quickly with their questioning, in situations such as this, to determine whether you have done your homework; they can make you quite unhappy if you have not!)

Here are some of the steps that have to be taken in automating a small office:

1. Design and specify the hardware elements (computer and peripheral devices such as printers, modems, switches, plotters, and so forth).
2. Choose and specify the necessary software programs.
3. Install and test the system, debugging as necessary.
4. Train the users.

Each step breaks down into various tasks. Other tasks that must be done (some directly related to the steps listed, others only indirectly related) are as follows:

- Perform trade-off studies, especially cost analyses of alternatives.
- Prepare formal reports for management review and evaluation.

- Develop precise specifications.
- Write custom software packages.
- Help recruit qualified computer operators.
- Provide turnkey services.
- Provide or arrange for maintenance services.
- Identify best sources of supply.
- Make formal presentations to management.

Proper planning includes anticipating and identifying all the needs, but, as you can see from a mere perusal of the items listed, most of them are beyond the abilities of anyone who is not reasonably expert with computers and computer systems. In fact, even trying to assemble that list might be beyond your own scope of knowledge, and it is possible that you would need a consultant to help you in the initial planning. That is an important lesson: Sometimes you need a consultant to help you determine whether you need a consultant!

Many consultants do not charge for a brief initial meeting, regarding it as a marketing function and thus an overhead expense. I follow that philosophy, as long as the meeting is local. Sometimes I have that initial meeting with a prospective client by telephone or by mail. In any case, the client and I each have our own objectives: The client wishes to determine whether he or she needs a consultant, and I wish to learn a bit more about what the need is and how good my chances are for landing the assignment. In that exchange, I inevitably give away some free consulting, and I determine what services I ought to offer.

It is perfectly legitimate for you, as a client or prospective client, to do this if the consultant is willing to cooperate. The consultant will help you identify your need more precisely than you have been able to and will suggest what services are best suited to that need. If you have had doubts as to whether you should retain a consultant, this becomes an aid to decision making.

WHAT ELSE YOU NEED TO KNOW

Decisions can never be better than the information upon which they are based, and bad decisions are probably as often the consequence of insufficient information as they are of bad information. To decide whether you need a consultant, you must know what kinds of consultants are available and what kinds of services they offer, as well as have an accurate understanding of your own need or problem. (You can hardly decide whether you need a security consultant if you are unaware that such consultants exist.)

The fact is that there are consultants in virtually every field of activity, including many that you have probably never considered. However, there are also distinctions in how consultants work or the kinds of services they offer.

A FEW BROAD CATEGORIES OF SERVICES AVAILABLE

As a simple example of broad distinctions in services, consider the differences among three general types of consultants: one offering diagnostic assistance, a second offering solution-design services, and a third offering solution-implementation services. To put it another way, consider the differences among (1) those whose service is based on pure knowledge, (2) those whose service is based on design talents, and (3) those whose service is based on personal skills. (Of course, there are also many consultants whose services include all these abilities and talents.)

For example, a general surgeon may call in a specialist to provide a second opinion, to help design a surgical strategy and procedure, or to perform the surgery. As another example—an actual case—a major computer manufacturer was unable to provide manuals that satisfied the customer, a branch of the

U.S. Navy. The Navy refused to pay the bill until satisfactory manuals were provided. The manufacturer called in a consulting firm to solve the problem. The manufacturer did not care to hear what was wrong with the manuals that had been rejected by the Navy, or even to review a corrective design, because they did not plan to have their in-house staff of engineers and writers make another try at satisfying the customer. They simply wanted the problem solved—the manuals made acceptable. In contrast, another client simply wanted expert service to analyze a request for proposals and brief his staff on the best strategy to use in bidding for a government contract. He called on a consultant to provide that advice—a hybrid of analysis and design service—alone.

In another, and perhaps more illuminating case, a bidder for sensitive military communications equipment had no one on staff who was expert enough in the specialized areas of EMP (the huge electromagnetic pulse that is generated during a nuclear detonation) and Tempest (protection of communications equipment from excessive radiation that would permit eavesdropping by hostile listeners) to propose design approaches for the bidder's proposal. The consultant specialist was expert enough in these areas but was not a writer. Therefore, a consultant specialist in proposal writing was also hired to rewrite the raw technical data supplied by the EMP/Tempest specialist and the other engineers.

DO YOU NEED EXPERT SKILLS OR EXPERT KNOWLEDGE?

The main point here is that some kinds of problems require specific skills, as well as knowledge, to solve them. As an illustration of this, a dentist I once knew was expert in dental technology and methods, and his office was always equipped with the most modern devices. But he was a bit clumsy, lacking in manual dexterity, so that his dental ministrations were almost always anticipated with apprehension and experienced with unhappiness. Referring back to the earlier example of the computer manufacturer, a consultant who can diagnose what is wrong with a set of manuals is not necessarily capable of doing an effective job of rewriting them. Hence the need to understand all the many definitions of consulting: If you are to be able to make sensible decisions about retaining consultants, you must know what is available to you and what you can and should seek, not only in terms of technical and professional specialties but also in terms of the kinds of services you can call for.

To even begin to analyze your own problem so that you can seek a solution, you must know what is available. The important arts of problem analysis and definition will be explored later in some detail as a necessary preliminary to beginning the quest for the right consulting services. You will then be in a far better position to perceive the importance of this understanding of what consultants are and how they function.

Another consideration is the length of time necessary to satisfy your need, for there are consultants who prefer long-term assignments and others who prefer short-term assignments. It is necessary to understand this characteristic when you find yourself in need of help.

That brings up the matter of a rather special type of consultant, the *technical/professional temporary.* Just as office temporaries—clerks, typists, stenographers, and other office help—are often made available on a short-term basis and paid, usually, by the hour, so are technical/professional specialists such as writers, editors, engineers, illustrators, and designers available as temporaries for both short- and long-term assignments. (Often supposedly short-term assignments go on and on, unexpectedly, and become long-term propositions running to many months and even several years.)

WHY AND WHEN TO TURN TO CONSULTING SERVICES

Finally, after all the discussions, what are the signs and signals that point to a possible need for consulting services? There are certain basic situations that ought to suggest the use of consulting services, at least as a possibility. At the minimum, those situations include the following:

- A problem that requires some highly specialized knowledge, skill, or experience for its solution
- A need to get a second opinion
- A temporary overload in requirements for technical/professional staff

The Requirement for Specialized Knowledge and Skills

Problems that require special abilities of some sort for their solution arise frequently today. The increasingly ubiquitous desktop computer alone spawns many such problems. Among the basic services computer specialists offer are studying typical office operations and recommending a system design, selecting hardware and software, getting the system set up, and training personnel. Even then there are specialties within specialties, for the computer field has grown too large and complex for any individual to be expert across the board in computers. Computer consultants generally list their areas of expertise in at least the areas of hardware (computer makes and models), computer languages, and level of expertise (i.e., programming, systems analysis, system design, etc). But many go well beyond that to list their special skills in applications such as inventory control, accounting and payroll, publishing, and other business applications.

It is probably obvious that you need help in such areas if you are not expert with computers. Even if you are, problems often arise that require some kind of skill or knowledge you either do not possess or do not possess at a sufficiently advanced level. However, there are many other areas in which your need for a consultant is far less obvious and you do not realize that a consultant can be a great asset or even that the subject is more complex than it appears to be. Here are just a few examples of such situations:

- If you do a great deal of mailing but are not well versed in mail systems, an expert is likely to be able to show you how to save a great deal of money. (The U.S. Postal Service will send out an expert to help you learn the most efficient ways to use the mails.)
- A consultant may be able to guide you to a more useful and less costly telephone system than you now have. There are consultants who specialize in this.
- Printing costs can vary widely, and if you spend a great deal of money every year on printing, retention of a printing expert may cut your costs significantly.
- Office efficiency has been raised considerably by consultants who design office systems and procedures. (The U.S. Energy Research and Development Administration, now part of the Department of Energy, hired a consultant to design a correspondence system for them when they found that their own methods bogged down.)
- Experts are available to consult in efficiency improvement. The Environmental Protection Agency ran into difficulties

in getting applications for civic water-treatment plants processed in time to spend the $10 billion in grant money authorized by Congress. EPA therefore hired a team of value engineers to study and improve the system. (Value engineers work at simplifying and improving designs and systems of all kinds.)

Alerting Signals

A question that probably arises in your mind as you read this is, How can I tell if my present equipment or system is not efficient and can be improved enough to justify hiring someone to do it? That is a fair question.

Probably the first signal that should alert you to the possibility is cost. Take a look at the various costs on your ledger. How much do you spend on telephone service? On postage? On delivery services? On clerical help? On insurance? Any item of high expenditure should become suspect; there is probably a way to reduce its cost.

You should review your costs from time to time and be alert to any items that regularly result in large annual expenditures. Be especially alert to sudden and/or sharp increases in any given cost area. Such increases should lead you to think about the possibility of finding someone who can (1) determine whether significant cost reductions can be made and (2) show you how to make them.

That is a conscious and deliberate effort. However, it is also possible to make that effort almost automatic and unconscious. You can condition yourself to become alert to cost-cutting possibilities to the point where you no longer think consciously about them but immediately take notice when you see high costs anywhere in your operation. When you see information bearing on cost reduction—learning of a consultant who specializes in some relevant area, for example—you pay attention to it.

That is easier to do than you might imagine. I was so pleased by the publication of my first book that I decided to write another. But on what? I had already written a book on the subject I knew best. After several aborted attempts to find a suitable new subject, I finally succeeded in writing a second book and having it published. Then I was stumped for a new idea about something within my own experience, but I struggled and finally found a suitable idea. The more I struggled consciously to get ideas, the more my subconscious mind began to help me by working on the problem and prompting me with periodic inspirations. Getting new book ideas has not been a serious problem since those early days. (In fact, my subconscious mind has suggested another book idea to me during the writing of this chapter.) Creativity and the subject of "inspirations" will be explored later.

Getting a Second Opinion

The patient faced with an ominous diagnosis and prognosis or a recommendation for a serious operation is quite likely to seek a second opinion and is wise to do so. Most physicians would agree that it is a good course of action and would themselves turn to a colleague for an opinion. This should not be confined to the practice of medicine; many so-called cures or other recommendations in business and industry should be received and/or followed up by getting a second, independent opinion. There are at least two cases in which it is wise to do so because the consequences of a mistake can be serious or even disastrous:

1. When the cost involved in the original recommendation or "opinion" is a large one
2. When the basic "health" of the organization can be seriously undermined by a bad decision

It is fairly easy to make this judgment when the first case prevails. In fact, caution is almost automatic when a relatively large amount of money is involved, whether the organization could afford the possible financial loss or not. No sensible executive spends large sums of money without careful consideration and study. (*Large* is, of course, a relative term and must be defined for your own purposes and circumstances. Certainly, it does not translate into the same numbers for General Motors as it does for Jones Software developers. But even in the case of General Motors or IBM, the term translates differently for the top executive in a major department than it does for a subordinate executive in a minor support department.)

The second case is less obvious, but it illustrates a sound principle of management and decision making in general: the need to make a worst-case and/or risk analysis. This is done by projecting or estimating the worst possible consequences of implementing the plan or making the investment you contemplate as representative of the first opinion. It is useful to estimate the probable risk in both qualitative and quantitative terms. Comparing what you stand to gain against what you may lose yields a qualitative analysis. Following that up with your best estimate in percentage terms of the possibilities of failure and success represents a quantitative analysis. These analyses—especially the worst-case analysis—are indicators of the importance of the decision. (Admittedly, these are difficult analyses to make, and they are largely dependent on individual judgment and therefore often influenced by emotional biases. However, it is far better to at least try to make an objective judgment than to react on a purely emotional basis. Moreover, you can greatly increase the probability of accuracy in your estimates and assessments by bringing others into the picture to make their own analyses and projections to be averaged with yours.)

Even a high-risk prospect is not forbidding if worst-case analysis reveals relatively little to lose, but a moderate risk is likely to be too great to undertake if the worst-case analysis suggests that you are gambling the future and possibly the very existence of the organization. The importance of performing these analyses to determine whether you should get a second opinion cannot be overstated.

Getting a second opinion—often many second opinions—is an automatic result when you issue a request for proposals. The relevance and value of the opinions embodied in the proposals, however, are most likely to be in some proportion to the care with which you have prepared the statement of work, the quality of the consultants from whom you solicit proposals, and your stated requirements for proposal content. Reading the proposals can often be an educational process in itself, helping you gain much greater insight into your own problems and needs, and to a large extent that result is magnified by the number of proposals you read. (One basic benefit of soliciting proposals is to help you weigh a number of approaches and credentials for getting the job done, so you normally want to attract more than one or two proposals.)

In any case, whether you call for formal proposals or not, it is wise to treat consultants' opinions very much as you would treat physicians' opinions. Bear in mind that you call for consulting services when you have an individual problem that requires individual problem solving, rather than a routine, off-the-shelf solution; therefore, it represents an individual's unique opinion and is not a tested solution. This advice is not necessarily confined to evaluating a first opinion from a professional consultant. That first opinion or original recommendation may have come to you from a dealer or supplier with whom you do business, a personal or business friend, someone on your own staff or within your own organization—perhaps an internal consultant—or even from a magazine article. Whatever its source, it should still be subject to the test of at least a second opinion before it is adopted, unless it concerns a trivial matter in which mistaken judgment or poor decisions cannot have disastrous results.

Handling Temporary Overloads

It usually costs a great deal of money to recruit new employees, especially those who are technical, professional, or even paraprofessional or subprofessional employees. In fact, the costs of full-scale recruiting are so high today that many employers pay professional recruiting firms placement fees of thousands of dollars for each new employee supplied, and some even offer existing employees substantial bonuses for bringing in acceptable new employees. Therefore, it is impractical to hire additional permanent employees for temporary overloads. It is almost always more economical to retain consultants who hire out as technical or professional temporaries, working on your own premises as though they were regular employees at an hourly or daily rate.

For example, the U.S. Postal Service, operating their then-new training division, hired a number of consultants on a long-term basis and continued to use consultants until they had reached the point at which they believed they knew just what their permanent staffing needs were. They then phased out the consultants and built up the permanent staff to the desired levels. Xerox Corporation established a training division in Leesburg, Virginia, and retained a number of consultants for a long term to develop their training programs. When the work was completed, the consultants were phased out. General Motors, establishing a training facility in Virginia, also employed consultants to get the staff of the facility organized and into operation.

HOW SPECIALIZED ARE THE CONSULTING SERVICES YOU NEED?

There is a limit to how specialized consultants and their services ought to be in practical terms. If specialization were carried to excess, it could mean that you would need several consultants to work on your problem, one for each of several aspects. On the other hand, you want someone who has considerably more than generalized knowledge of the subject. By definition, a consultant must have special capabilities.

Consultants are faced with the same problem from their own viewpoint. They must be specialized and yet not so specialized that the number of potential clients is unacceptably small. To survive, consultants must set their degree of specialization at a point that is compatible with the market for their services. From your viewpoint as a potential client, you must consider just how specialized the services you need really are and how difficult or unusual your problem is.

An Inherent Anomaly

There is a built-in anomaly in the very idea that a consultant must be a specialist, and this is especially true if the consultant is an independent practitioner rather than a member of a sizeable organization. The anomaly is this: In most cases a consultant must be reasonably proficient as an analyst, diagnostician, speaker, and writer, and if the consultant is an independent practitioner, he or she must also be proficient in typical business practices such as contract negotiation, pricing, and other everyday chores of business.

The Need for Oral and Written Presentations

One thing many clients overlook is their need for good documentation and effective oral presentations to higher-level management that explains the program for which the consultant was hired. These matters may well prove to be of direct and serious concern to you as the client, and you must consider them when defining what your needs are and seeking a consultant to help satisfy them. For example, it may be necessary for the consultant to make a stand-up presentation to a group of executives instead of or as a follow-up to the proposal; that is not an unusual requirement in many organizations. From your own viewpoint, as the executive who proposes to retain the consultant, you may need the help of the consultant in "selling" your decision to others in your organization. You also may need to have your consultant make such presentations as verbal progress reports and/or a final report. Therefore, since it may prove to be important to you to find a consultant who is capable of making good verbal presentations, it is a matter to consider as part of your planning.

Much the same considerations apply with regard to the writing abilities of consultants. Whether a consultant is or is not required to make stand-up presentations, it is almost an unvarying fact that written presentations are required in the form of progress reports and/or a final report. Your own reputation may depend on the quality of that writing. In many cases, the written report is the sole tangible product of all the dollars spend for the consulting service; it is therefore the only thing by which others will judge the quality of the service and your own performance in sponsoring it.

Chapter Three

Identifying the Problem and Defining the Need

Difficulty in identifying and defining "the problem" is a most common problem itself, as many consultants and other troubleshooters know.

THE COMMON DILEMMA OF PROBLEM/NEED DEFINITION

Preparing to retain a consultant, especially analyzing your situation to decide just what you need in the way of expert help, is admittedly not always an easy task. It is, in fact, among the management dilemmas referred to in the first chapter. Managers and consultants can attest to that from personal experience.

Over a large number of years spent in responding to calls from organizations requesting consulting help with bids, proposals, and other marketing activity, I have been surprised again and again to discover that quite often my prospective clients cannot define or identify their problems accurately. That is, their statements of work tend to have one or more of the following characteristics:

- The statement is specific, but it describes symptoms, rather than problems.
- The statement rambles vaguely and is less than specific even with respect to symptoms.
- The statement is quite specific, but it describes what often proves to be an imaginary problem, missing the real problem entirely.
- The statement admits—usually tacitly and by implication, rather than specification—total uncertainty as to the problem.

In all but the last case, the client usually believes firmly that he or she has provided all the necessary pertinent information and has identified or defined the problem that requires solution. That kind of failure has ill effects of several kinds. However, it is necessary to digress here for a moment to define a few terms so as to avoid confusion: The word *problem* is used here partly because of a common (albeit mistaken) belief that consulting always involves analyzing and solving a problem that the client does not know how to solve, but partly also for convenience, as a generic term. You may read *need* or *requirement* in place of *problem;* the terms are interchangeable in these pages. However, none of these terms fits all cases, and they also may be ambiguous. For example, a *requirement* is what the client's work statement describes as his or her need, but it may not be what the consultant perceives as the true need, and so it does not always refer literally to what the client has called for.

PROBLEM DEFINITION

Problem definition is a separate and distinct process that must be recognized as such if it is to be conducted efficiently. Many problems are readily apparent and may be identified and defined spontaneously, without formal or organized effort. But many others do not fit that description; they can be identified and defined only as a result of deliberate effort. Moreover, even when definitions appear to be obvious they can be deceptive. For example, when you need some extra help—perhaps a packaging designer to design a package for a new perfume—are you sure that you can define that need adequately? Let us examine the need.

The product is a new one with a new name. It is upscale, will be sold in department stores and other suitable emporia, and will be the forerunner of an entire new line if it is successful in the marketplace. It is a new departure for your company—a more upscale (expensive) product than you have manufactured and marketed before—and you are convinced that you ought to get a real specialist to design the package.

It seems simple enough: You need a packaging design for your new perfume, and the package must meet the following needs:

1. It must be of high enough quality for an upscale market; this is not a cheap scent. The package must impress department store buyers as well as individual customers.
2. It must be suitable for an entire line of cosmetic products, which will be launched if the perfume is successful enough. The motif and theme of the package must be easily transferrable to the packaging of toilet water, powder, soap, lotions, lipsticks, rouge, and other cosmetics, and possibly to cosmetic appliances as well.

Even with these needs defined, some questions remain: What is a "package"? Is it the carton in which the product is encased? Or does it include the container—the bottle or vial, in the case of the perfume, but the jars, tubes, boxes, and other containers for the companion cosmetics. Does that cover it? Or is a *package* also the entire advertising and promotion campaign—the *image* created for the line—as many marketing experts would insist?

By now it is apparent that designing a package is not as simple as it appears, and certainly finding the right consultant expert to do the job is not going to be simple. For example, can you use someone who has been packaging appliances for a living? Would he or she be able to package perfume adequately? Just what is a packaging designer, anyway? What does *packaging* mean, for that matter? Remember, the package must be such that it can be adapted to an entire line of cosmetics if this perfume takes off and is successful. Moreover, it must be suitable for an upscale clientele.

Maybe there is no such thing as a packaging designer who specializes in cosmetics packaging. Perhaps the closest thing you can get is a consultant who designs shipping cartons or front panels for electronic appliances. Maybe you need to hire a firm, rather than an individual consultant. Or maybe you need to hire both: the firm to design the package and the individual consultant (a marketing professional) to represent you and ensure that the firm does a proper job.

It may appear, on casual inspection, that there is little or no difference between identification and definition of a problem. But, in fact, they are entirely different matters. For one thing, while you may have decided what the problem is as far as you are concerned—you have *identified* it accurately, in your own mind, that is—you must define it so that anyone you charge with solving the problem (a consultant, in this case) understands clearly what the problem is. I know at least one individual involved in hiring consultants who is quite bright but sadly lacking in the ability to communicate his thoughts clearly to others. I have found it necessary to be very careful in acting on his definitions by taking careful, sometimes extraordinary steps to ensure that I understand not only what he is saying but also what he *thinks* he is saying. This is not uncommon. Anyone who reads and attempts to respond to requests for proposals and work statements issued by government offices has encountered numerous difficulties of this kind, sometimes dismissed as "governmentese" or "bureaucratese" (inflated writing) but more often the result of fuzzy, undisciplined thinking.

It is an excellent idea to write out your definition of the problem or need simply to clarify your own thinking. You may very well find it difficult to describe the problem in writing. That is a clear indication that you have not thought it out and identified it as clearly as you should have or thought you had. Your ability to explain your concept in words (and possibly in charts or drawings) is both an acid test of your own understanding and an excellent medium to help you think things out in detail and thereby improve your understanding.

It should be clear now that identifying your problem or need is not precisely the same as defining it, although both terms have been used to highlight the problem of vague and uncertain statements of need. *Identifying* means recognizing your need accurately, while *defining* it is explaining it to prospective consultants so that they understand it exactly as you do. Failure in either area can frustrate your objectives and lead to failed or at least seriously flawed projects. There are several kinds of mistakes clients commonly make in both identifying and defining their needs. The following are probably the most common:

- Mistaking symptoms for problems
- Making faulty deductions
- Compromising both definition and solution by making assumptions about the solution in the statement of the problem
- Making other nonsequiturs and related logical anomalies

Mistaking Symptoms for Problems

This is a common error. A surprisingly large number of people are either unable or unwilling to distinguish between a problem and its symptoms. They are unable to analyze a condition beyond the rough discriminations that are usually fairly obvious on even casual examination and consideration. Presumably, not everyone has the instinctive ability to conduct an analysis and make fine discriminations, that is, to make accurate diagnoses. Diagnostics calls for an ability to make those fine discriminations and to perceive the entire chain of logic between causes and effects, discriminating carefully between the two in each case, and tracing the chain of causes and effects back to the first or original cause. Thus, diagnostic ability is a talent in itself, one that is useful to clients and consultants alike.

An Example

One client, who explained that his problem was that his computer produced inaccurate and untimely reports, was describing a symptom but identifying it as a problem. Of course, from his viewpoint as a manager in need of accurate reports, he simply was not interested in, nor did he perceive a need for, analyzing the process to identify the true problem. After all, he reasoned, that was why he had called for proposals to help him choose the right consultant expert. Pressed hard enough, he undoubtedly would have admitted that his description of the problem to be solved was not totally accurate. The true problem was not the faulty reports, of course; it was probably one or more of the following three possibilities:

1. Hardware defects (the equipment was unreliable)
2. Software defects (there were logical or functional flaws in the programs)
3. Input defects (poor information was being supplied to the system)

The first possibility was unlikely, although not impossible. Computer hardware generally tends to be reliable. In any case, hardware problems almost surely would have manifested themselves in other ways also.

The second suggested cause was quite possible; for a variety of reasons, a great deal of the software we use does far less than we wish it to do, so it is usually a plausible suspect.

The third possibility was also entirely possible. The systems used to collect information for computer processing might very well have been less than optimal for the task, even if some experienced professional had designed the system. Even if the system design—the forms and the methods for collecting and recording data—were faultless, the operation or actual collection might have been carried out carelessly, thus defeating an excellent design. That, too, is well within the realm of what happens quite commonly.

Making Faulty Deductions

Problem identification is, of course, a logical process, as the example used here should show. It requires identification of a cause-effect relationship, with the cause usually representing the problem while the effect represents the symptom. Usually, logical analysis produces a list of *possible* causes, as in the example. That is not always the case, however; sometimes it is possible to gather enough information from simple observation of symptoms to identify the first cause or true problem reliably. In any case, analysis of symptoms (effects) and probable causes ought to be pursued as far as possible in preparing a description of the problem.

Compromising the Definition

The client who confines the work statement to a description of the problem and/or symptoms, without suggesting an approach to a solution, is probably acting wisely in most cases. Suggesting a solution or approach to a solution quite often represents leaping to a conclusion or otherwise having a biased view that compromises the integrity of the work statement. Several years ago, the Post Office Department (before it became a government corporation identified as the U.S. Postal Service) wished to retain the services of a consulting firm to handle a variety of tasks connected with its mainframe computers at Paramus, New Jersey. However, Post Office officials made the mistake of specifying a solution approach in their request for proposals. That imposed a difficult, if not impossible, requirement because it called for capabilities that few, if any, computer consultants had. This limited the response severely, and it compelled proposers to stretch the facts.

The work statement should include as much information as possible about the problem, its symptoms, and the client's relevant needs and conditions, but it should leave to the consultants the job of proposing.

Making Other Nonsequiturs and Anomalies

Unfortunately, other anomalies of various kinds tend to creep into descriptions of the problem and what is to be done. These include excursions into indirectly related and even unrelated areas, as well as other distractors that compromise the integrity of the statement and, indeed, of the entire program. Rigid editing, with scrupulous discard of irrelevant material, can spell an end to most such problems in work statements.

CAN WE DEFINE THE VERY WORD *PROBLEM?*

One thing to learn from the example cited here is that there is no reliable universal or absolute definition of the idea that the word *problem* represents. How one identifies something as a problem depends in large part on the individual's perspective, and that in turn often depends on the individual's position, responsibility, or other special interest. In example, the faulty reports were a *management* problem, from the manager's viewpoint. However, the consultant retained as a systems expert would be more likely to regard it, even on the scant information suggested here, as a computer systems problem. If a computer programmer were included in this discussion, he or she would be likely to regard it as a software problem. And anyone in charge of collecting the data would likely think immediately in terms of doing something about the forms and/or data-gathering processes.

An individual's relative position in the hierarchy can affect how he or she defines a condition as a "problem." For example, the president of a firm calls in the vice president in charge of production and says, "Pete, we have a problem here. Customers are complaining about late shipments. Get on it, please, and straighten it out."

Pete now goes to his production manager and says, "Joe, we have a problem. The prez is after me about complaints from customers of late shipments. What about it? Why are the shipments late? Get on it!"

Joe Production Manager says, "Whoa! Wait a minute! There is no delay in production. We're not the problem. Maybe you need to talk to shipping."

Harry Head Shipper says, "Not us, pardner; we're not your problem. It must be UPS. We ship every order the day received."

And so on, down the line, until the true first cause is discovered.

Flexibility of the Definition

Notice that the definition of the problem changes constantly according to individual circumstances and considerations. Certainly it is not news that most of us strongly tend to define a problem in terms of our own direct interests and to think of solutions with that same perspective and orientation. The consultant, especially the consultant who is called upon to solve problems that require analysis and deductive reasoning, must learn to apply a sterner discipline to his or her thinking than is usually required of the client.

Few people naturally tend to see a problem as others do, for obvious reasons. Self-defense is one such reason, but in many cases the reason is merely the orientation the individual has due to position or profession: It simply does not occur to him or her that there are other viewpoints and orientations. For example, the diplomat tends to think that war can be prevented by international pacts and disarmament, but the military leader thinks that war can best be prevented by mutual assured destruction, sheer weight of arms, and/or first-strike capability. There are aspirants to leadership who espouse the idea of one-world government as their standard for peace on the planet. They believe that their ideas are *new, bold,* and *different,* and thus are more effective definitions of and solutions to the problems of international rivalry and war.

Mutuality of Need

It is self-defeating for the client to overlook the consultant's perspective when explaining or describing a problem. There are at least two possible undesirable consequences of a faulty statement of the problem:

1. The consultant may take the statement at face value, develop a proposed service based on an inaccurate or incomplete problem description, and deliver an unsatisfactory performance as a result.
2. The consultant may perform an independent analysis, make arbitrary assumptions, build into his or her program a requirement for independent initial problem definition, and price it accordingly (i.e., on the high side) to play it safe.

Actually, there is a third possibility, even more undesirable from both the consultant's and the client's viewpoint: Faced with the problem of trying to be competitive in price with others, the consultant is often reluctant to opt for the second alternative suggested here because that approach tends to drive the cost estimate up. There is a strong temptation, therefore, to opt for the first choice, even bidding a deliberately unrealistically low figure, with the expectation of "getting well" (renegotiating the contract) later, when it becomes apparent that the original statement of work was faulty and the consultant cannot be held responsible for the need to redo the work. This is not an uncommon ploy in some of the more competitive consulting specialties, and it clearly demonstrates why it is very much in the client's interest to be sure that the problem statement is accurate in all respects.

Suppose You Cannot Identify the Problem

None of this is to say that it is always possible for you, the client, to identify and define the core problem; frequently, it is not. (Frequently, in fact, you would not need the consultant at all if you could identify the problem!) It is not absolutely necessary to identify the problem in such cases, but *you must be aware that you do not know what the problem is*, and you must conceive and structure your request for proposals accordingly. That is, you must make it plain that you are describing symptoms and, possibly, history and other relevant facts and that at least part of the service you require is a study to identify and define the problem.

This is why many clients retain a consultant to write or help in writing the request for proposals—especially the statement of work—to ensure accuracy. It is better to retain a consultant to do this work as a separate, preliminary project, rather than as a phase of a larger program, because it is difficult to project costs before the true problem has been identified and because you retain a greater measure of control by handling it in this way. (Moreover, in some cases it is quite possible that you could do the rest of the work yourself.)

Recognizing a Proper Definition

In discussing the difficulties of identifying and defining problems, I have posed a dilemma: the difficulty of knowing when a problem has been defined properly—that is, when a direct cause, rather than an effect or a symptom, has been identified. How can you be sure that you are not confusing problems with their symptoms? Admittedly, it is not always easy to make this discrimination, but there is one guideline that has proved to be quite reliable: The problem has been identified when it contains within its definition a direct clue to the solution, to a set of probable solutions, or (at least) to a direct approach to a solution. The example posed earlier, in which the computer turned out unreliable reports, will illustrate this.

In this simple case, there were two real possibilities: The software was at fault or the input data were at fault. Even when one or the other possibility has been confirmed the core problem has not yet been identified, for each of these possibilities has subsets that must be examined.

If it is determined that the software is at fault, it may be that a bad choice of off-the-shelf software was made or someone did a poor job of writing custom software. That means that better proprietary software should be sought out, if any such software exists that would be right for this need. Or it may be that using off-the-shelf software was the bad decision and custom software should have been written. On the other hand, if the software was custom-written for the application, the nature of its faults must be made clear before the problem can be identified as a need to write a new program or do corrective work on the existing program.

Obviously, there are great cost differentials involved here, so it is important to know enough about the problem to know what the possible solutions are.

The same range of possibilities exists with respect to data-input faults: The system for gathering the data, the forms used, and the quality of the work in gathering the data and/or transcribing it are all possible causes, but each has a different route to solution and a different price tag, hence the need to know as exactly as possible just what will be required.

But there are no absolutes here either: What is a direct cause or what indicates a solution or solution approach can also vary in terms of the individual's special interests. The general manager, faced with customer complaints of delay in deliveries, wants only to find out which of his subordinate managers is responsible for the cause of the delays: Is it in the production department or the shipping department? Beyond that, it is the relevant subordinate manager's problem; the general manager has identified the problem as far as his role and responsibility are concerned. (The general manager is not and should not ordinarily be concerned with mechanical breakdowns, excessive absenteeism, poor services by common carriers, or other problems that arise at subordinate levels.) The same considerations apply to the solution, which is obvious in this case: Immediately order the responsible manager to straighten the trouble out.

Thus, even problem definitions and problem solutions exist in hierarchies, and you must make that clear in your own mind and in your statement of work to prospective consultants.

Given a properly written statement of work, one that makes it clear that it does not attempt to define the problem but includes useful information such as a complete description of symptoms, history, efforts made to date, and other data, the capable consultant will perform as much preliminary analysis as possible on the basis of what is provided. He or she will normally propose some specific course of action, depending on that evaluation. The proposed program may be a solution if the consultant is confident that the analysis has identified the problem. (Ordinarily, the proposal will present the proposer's definition of the problem, or it should do so.) Otherwise, the consultant is likely to propose a program of study to undertake such an identification as a first phase of effort. It will be your responsibility, of course, to decide whether the proposal is satisfactory and merits an award and go-ahead. That is, you should verify that the consultant has defined the problem, that the definition offered makes sense to you and you can accept it, and that the proposal describes a specific course of action to solve the problem and shows clearly that the proposed course of action is a logical extension of the problem statement.

PROBLEM ANALYSIS

None of this is intended to diminish the importance of doing as much analysis of your own as possible. The more you know about the problem from your own experience and effort, the more confidence you will have in any program you agree to, the greater the probability that the program will be successful and satisfying, and the greater your control over the program.

Remember here that the word *problem* does not necessarily refer to a dilemma or a technical question that you do not know how to solve; you may know very well how to solve it. In other words, your problem may be simply how to *best* satisfy a well-defined need or where to get the most effective service. You may know, for example, that you need the services of a financial expert to work in your own offices for a period of several weeks to prepare a plan for financing a merger. Your problem is then one of finding the financial consultant who is likely to be most satisfactory to you in terms of cost, relevant experience, personality characteristics, and other such matters.

Whether you have a technical problem that requires specialized skills and knowledge to solve or a need that is more in keeping with this latter description, there are helpful methods to aid you in making an analysis and identifying or defining the problem and finding solutions.

A First Step

As a first step in making an analysis, you need to decide at what level you wish to have the problem identified. That means asking and getting answers to certain questions. The following are among the types of questions to be asked. (Select those most appropriate to your situation.)

1. For whom is this service to be performed?
2. Who will put the resulting information or service to use?
3. To what use will the resulting information or service be put?

This is a critical first area to think about in deciding *what* problem is to be identified. If you want to know only whether the problem of faulty reports from the computer is a computer-program problem or a data-input problem (i.e., you want to know only who you must consult to get the end-problem solved), you do not care to know how data-collection forms should be designed or what the common faults in report generators are. Those are matters for someone else to be concerned with. However, if you are the "someone else"—the manager who is directly responsible for the reports, for example—you will want ideas and information at a lower and more detailed level. So it is necessary for you to have a clear idea of the answers to both the first and second questions.

The question of what use the resulting information will be put to is relevant here, too. The information might be used to decide whether to take the next step (correcting the problem) in house, with staff people, or by contracting out to some other consultant specialist. On the other hand, if there is already an advance decision that the corrective work, whatever it proves to be, will be done in house, that tells you that you need a final report that is diagnostic enough to guide the in-house staff in correcting the problem.

You can see that these matters are interrelated: The answer to one question may affect the answer to another.

Some Basic Injunctions

It is important that analysis be objective if it is to be maximally useful. A general rule that must be applied to make analyses as objective as possible is *the verb-noun rule:* Use only verbs and nouns to answer questions. Adding adjectives and adverbs strongly tends to reduce the level of objectivity and introduce an undesirable subjectivity. For example, answering the first question (For whom is this service to be performed?) with "The Comptroller, Heavy Equipment Division" is considerably different in its connotations and total impact from "The Comptroller responsible for accuracy in Heavy Equipment Division accounting reports." The latter statement is likely to color the interpretation of the need. It therefore helps to use the most objective of terms—unmodified verbs and nouns.

This discussion serves primarily to alert you to the basic need for thoughtful analysis and the hazards of making careless assumptions. Much more detailed discussions of these matters will be provided in a later section dealing with specific procedures for developing statements of work to use in issuing requests for proposals.

BORROWINGS FROM A CONSULTING DISCIPLINE

Disproportions between percentages of input and output are not unique to any field; they are common and were rediscovered in the development of the discipline known variously as *value engineering*, *value analysis*, and, more recently, *value management*, itself a consulting specialty. The basic lessons and methodology of the discipline can be applied to choosing and using consultants effectively. But before that is addressed directly, another digression is necessary to examine the discipline briefly and understand its fundamentals.

Value management, or VM as it is referred to here, is a management discipline that originally grew out of and was applied to engineering applications but more recently has been extrapolated and generalized to other applications as the universality of its messages and usefulness has become apparent. In its engineering applications, VM simplifies designs and processes, reducing costs without sacrificing quality or usefulness. It does this through a most logical and sensible attack.

THE ESSENCE OF VALUE MANAGEMENT

In its essence, VM answers just two important questions:

1. Precisely what is it that the item (machine, process, system, person, etc.) does, is supposed to do, or is intended to do as its true, main, or primary function?
2. What is the most effective, efficient, and/or economical way to carry out that true, main, or primary function?

The entire discipline is designed to get dependable and sensible answers to these two questions.

Stated baldly, as these questions are here, the answers might appear to be childishly simple to reach. However, this is deceptive: Even the first question is quite often a difficult one to answer reliably. The VM discipline is designed specifically to elicit accurate answers to both questions, but especially to the first.

Identifying Functions

It has been found in conducting VM training that many learners are intimidated, even mystified, by the word *function*. People who are not engineers tend to see it as a formidable technical term, possibly because so many VM instructors are engineers schooled in the discipline *VE—value engineering.* Yet, no good substitute has been found for the word *function,* and it has a significance that is at the heart of the discipline: Value management is about function—about *main* or *primary* functions and about *support* and *secondary* or *ancillary* functions.

Function is not a technical word. It refers simply to what something *does* or *should do.* The real problem in defining functions is the need for highly disciplined reasoning. As an object lesson in this, try your hand at defining the function of a lead pencil. Stop reading for a moment and ponder this—defining what it does or should do—before you go on.

If you are typical of most people who encounter VM for the first time, you have decided that the function of a lead pencil is to write. That is an understandable error because writing is the *use* most of us make of a pencil. But that is *not* what a pencil *does:* The pencil does not write; humans write. A pencil merely *makes marks,* whatever marks the user wants it to make. In fact, in many cases the user is not writing at all, but merely making marks, as when a technician or mechanic uses a pencil to mark off a dimension or when an illustrator makes a sketch.

Inevitably, when this is used as a basic example, someone will point out that many pencils have erasers and so have a second function, to remove marks. That is true, of course, but it is also true that the eraser is a *secondary* function. Moreover, it is not a *support* function—that is, it is independent of the main function of making marks and is in no way necessary to that main function. Without the eraser, the pencil still makes marks.

Secondary Functions

Many items have more than one function. It is necessary to decide what the main or primary function is, but it is also necessary to identify all secondary functions and to determine whether the secondary functions are also support functions.

A secondary function is a support function if it is necessary to the primary function, rather than ancillary to it—if, that is, the primary function could not be accomplished without the secondary function. The checkwriter could not accomplish its primary function of safeguarding checks without performing the secondary functions of writing checks and perforating paper. On the other hand, a tie clip has a primary function of securing a tie and a secondary function of being decorative, but the secondary function is purely ancillary and does not support the primary function: The tie clip would secure the tie whether it was also decorative or not.

This is not to derogate or discount the intrinsic value of a tie clip as jewelry, for that is also an authentic value. However, recognizing that its decorative value is a secondary function puts it into proper perspective and acknowledges what is fact in the quest for truth and efficiency. The significance of this process in choosing and using consultants will soon be apparent, if it is not already.

The Verb-Noun Rule

One way VM forces disciplined thinking on its practitioners is via the verb-noun rule, which states that function must be defined with a single verb and a single noun. Occasionally a compound verb or noun is required as an exception to the rule, but the philosophy and purpose are the same: to establish and maintain objectivity, which is immediately threatened by adjectives and adverbs. Another example will be useful here.

The checkwriting machine that many businesses employ to impress the amount on the check with perforations and color is a case in point. What is the main function of this device? "To write checks," you say? So do many other newcomers to VM, until they have learned the discipline of objective analysis. It would be as easy to write a check by hand or by typewriter and avoid the cost of the machine. Why use a special machine? The answer is that the function is to *safeguard checks*. That is, checks are quite difficult to alter when processed through such a machine.

The way to reach that conclusion is simple enough: Ask yourself a question: What is the *purpose* of the item? *Why* does it exist? What makes it necessary? What is its *mission* or the *reason* for its existence?

It is not always easy to reason out answers to such questions because not all cases are straightforward and simple. In one case, even the VM instructors were at a loss for a while when asked to define the main function of an overhead projector. Their spontaneous reaction was to say, "It projects images," just as neophytes are usually inspired to use the generic descriptor of the item in defining its function. But when they stopped to analyze the reason for its existence, the mystery was cleared up. The overhead projector is used by presenters to enable everyone in an audience to see something together. In this case, the function is *achieved* by enlarging and projecting an image, but that is irrelevant to the present discussion. The main function is to *present images*, regardless of the mechanical means for doing so.

AN IMPORTANT APPLICATION

To get a bit closer to one of the most important kinds of uses that can be made of this logical discipline in choosing and using consultants, this kind of reasoning will now be applied to the case of a human being performing a job. What is (or should be) the main function of a secretary? Making coffee? Typing letters? Making copies? Filing papers? Answering telephones? Making reservations? Arranging travel? Making appointments? There is no doubt that secretaries do all of these things. Is any one of them a main secretarial function—that is, does one duty define the purpose of the job itself?

The answer is *no,* of course. Secretaries usually perform a variety of duties, including many or even all of the above. This shows that secretaries are rarely employed efficiently and that the qualifications for true secretarial competence are rarely defined. Consider, for example, how many of the duties just listed could be handled easily by someone paid less than a secretary. That alone suggests the need for a more sensible analysis and function definition than is usually employed.

The so-called "school solution" (my solution, that is) is this: A secretary is or should be employed for one main function only: to *save the executive's time.* The executive is highly paid and should not type, make copies, or answer routine telephone calls. Lesser-paid people relieve the executive of these types of chores so the executive can concentrate on work that justifies an exalted salary. Thus, the secretary screens telephone calls, makes travel reservations, screens the incoming mail, and performs other such duties. A file clerk makes coffee and runs errands, and a pool typist types correspondence. This is not a new or different concept; it is merely sensible management, assuming that one goal of management is the most efficient use of all resources, including personnel. It is an organized system to force intelligent analysis of designs, processes, and anything else that costs money, time, and effort. It is entirely pragmatic in all its applications, and its goal is to establish truth and maximum efficiency.

In its most common use, VM is applied to evaluate and simplify designs by eliminating unnecessary functions and materials, thus reducing costs. (Its development was inspired as a direct result of a phenomenon observed during World War II, when a manager observed that sometimes a substitute material, used as an improvisation because of wartime shortage of the favored material, actually performed better and cost less than the material for which it was substituted.) Among the other critical questions to which answers are sought is "What does it cost?" That question is asked with regard to the original item, the original materials and methods, and all possible alternative materials and methods. The quest is to find alternatives that work as well as or better than the original ones but are less costly to find alternatives that, while they are not less costly, produce far better results—another way of increasing value.

WHAT IS VALUE?

Value is never easy to define, and the concept of what value is is at the heart of the discipline. The overall objective is to increase value. At least that was the original idea, although the concepts have developed and become a bit more sophisticated over the years.

Can We Manage Value?

In its most basic frame of reference, increasing value is simply getting more for the dollar. Value, then, represents a ratio between function and cost, and the nominal objective is to improve that ratio as far as possible: to get the greatest amount of function for the cost. But that proposition is not as straightforward as it appears to be, for there are at least two problems associated with it:

1. It is usually easy to quantify cost, because it is usually expressed in terms of dollars, labor hours, time, or some other easily measurable factor, but it is not always easy to quantify functional result. In fact, it is often quite difficult to do so.

2. There is a point of diminishing returns with function, in many cases. To increase functional effectiveness beyond that which is useful or necessary to produce the desired result is wasteful, so simply adding functional effectiveness is not the same thing as increasing value. To the extent that functional result can be quantified, either by measure or by estimate, there should be a cutoff point, a point at which more is not a benefit.

Value Is Not an Absolute

Obviously, then, value is not a constant or absolute; it is inevitably dependent on need and application. In fact, determining the wastefulness that results from excessive result—result beyond that which is needed—is itself one of the objectives of value studies. Many items are overdesigned and do more than the user needs, thereby wasting money. That is as true for systems, methods, processes, and job descriptions as it is for material products. (Overdesigning or designing for more result than is necessary to meet the original need is analogous to doubling the dosage recommended by the physician with the hope that recovery will be twice as rapid.)

Value does not have a single definition, for it is a relative quantity, not an absolute one. There are several kinds of value, so it can be a most elusive item to define, as in the case of the tie clip, where it became necessary to discriminate between practical functional value and esteem value. In practice, several kinds of value ordinarily must be defined:

1. Esteem value or what human beings, as individuals or as a class, consider some item to be worth. Art objects and antiques are good examples of this.
2. Functional value, or the worth of the item as a useful,

practical object—an electric drill or coffeemaker, for example.

3. Intrinsic value, or the worth of the item without regard to its esteem value or other qualities—for example, the worth of the precious stones set in a ring without regard to the ring's esteem value, or of the gold contained in an electronic device regardless of the functional value attached to the device.
4. Market value, which is often synonymous with one or more of the other values but must be recognized as a factor and considered nevertheless. (Items may have more than one value, for example, both esteem and intrinsic values.)

For the most part, this discussion is concerned with determining functional and market values and applying value management to choosing and using consultants and consulting services, but esteem value sometimes plays a part in this process, too, and it is impossible to ignore it entirely. The cost of a consultant's time—the value of his or her services—often depends at least partially on esteem value.

This might be labeled *market* value, rather than *esteem* value, since they are essentially the same thing in the case of consultants. That is, there are situations in which some consultants are normally able to command significantly higher fees than their fellows who offer essentially the same services. Where the market for a particular kind of consultant is perhaps $500 a day, there are often consultants offering those services who are able to command $1,000 or more per day because of their reputation. The market for the services of those consultants is special, based on the esteem in which they are held.

That special value depends on the perception of the buyers in the particular market, as exemplified in the market for works of art. As long as there are buyers who will pay the special rates asked by a consultant, those rates will remain the market value for that consultant's services. Are those fair and reasonable rates? Are the services provided by that consultant worth more to you than those provided by his or her competitors? That is a question you must answer for yourself, but the analytical discipline of value management is usually helpful in determining what is a fair value, at least in the most practical terms. In the case hypothesized here, you would attempt to find out why the services of the high-priced consultant were deemed to be worth more than those of competing consultants, and thus be able to determine the consultant's value to you—value for your application or need, that is. It is possible that the characteristic that makes the consultant's services especially valuable to others has no relevance to your own need.

This case illustrates another significant point made earlier: Value is not necessarily an absolute or fixed quantity, but may vary from one application to another or from one individual to another. Value must be determined in some relevant frame of reference, at least in the applications of concern here.

THE RELEVANCE OF VALUE MANAGEMENT

Value management is a useful management tool generally. However, it has at least a threefold relevance to the process of choosing and using consultants:

1. The accurate identification and definition of need is a must for sensible selection of the right kind of consulting help; hence the need for objective analysis of problems and needs.
2. Given the typical problem of choosing among competitors, some objective system of analysis is necessary to evaluate

the several contenders and their proposals in order to make a choice.

3. Finally, even after these two problems have been surmounted, some reasonably objective system for evaluating the consultant's performance is necessary.

The objective of analysis described so briefly here satisfies these needs in all respects, as will become evident in later discussions of its methods and applications.

USING THE VM APPROACH

Assume that you have a need to design a product package using the value management approach. First, you try to find out something about the package:

1. *What is it?*
   A package.
   Well, you knew that. That's only a name.
2. *What does it do?*
   Contains/presents product.
   Oh, it *presents* the product? That means it is a *marketing matter*, does it not?

Now that casts an entirely new light on the subject. Perhaps you had not thought of the package as part of the marketing consideration, but of course it is. You can see that now. A packaging consultant must be someone with a marketing sense, perhaps a marketer who specializes in packaging.

Go back and study this some more. *Presents product* is the main or primary function, but there may be other functions, secondary ones. You can go back to VM to explore those:

3. *What else does it do?*
   Distinguishes product.
   Establishes identity.
   Creates theme.
   Supports image.

Refining the Definition

Translating these secondary functions, you confirm that a *package* in this case is not the mere box and wrappings, nor even the bottle or tube in which it is enclosed: It is the entire *image* with which the product is endowed—it is packaging in the advertising and public relations (PR) sense. So packaging is really part of the marketing operation, thus it ought to be the responsibility of the person who handles marketing. Now you are beginning to get a little more insight into what is needed in the way of consulting skills—not an industrial engineer, whom you might retain to design purely physical packaging such as cartons and Styrofoam forms, but a marketing specialist who understands *packaging* in the far more global sense of marketing needs—advertising and PR, in this case.

Differences in Definitions

This is unlike the case of Aspen Ribbons, Inc., a company that paid $5,000 to a packaging consultant when they realized that they were actually losing money because of inefficient *physical* packaging. In that case, the package was not especially significant to the marketing activity, and the term *package* was used in its most literal sense. This is another example of how different the meaning of a term can be in different applications and different contexts.

The key, then, is the *function analysis*. And in this case you applied the analysis of *What is it?* and *What does it do?* to an abstract concept, *packaging*, rather than to a physical item or system. You started with an understandable assumption, a "draft definition" of packaging as a process of creating the physical container and wrappings to be used in connection with the product. But value analysis led swiftly to a considerable degree of enlightenment and refinement of the definition, and that led to a much different view of what kind of consultant was needed.

MAXIMIZING THE USEFULNESS OF VALUE MANAGEMENT

Historically, value analyses have been applied to existing items, and sometimes the cost of the analytical effort has been greater than the cost of redesigning the item or, in the case of manufactured items, the cost of retooling has been greater than the savings that would be realized through redesign. That is an inevitable consequence of ex post facto value analysis: It is all too often a case of the ancient platitude about locking the barn door after the horse has been stolen.

To be maximally useful, value management ought to be carried out as part of the original planning and preparation for a task. You should seek definitions and insights—carry out the value analysis—*before* making final decisions. Value analysis is a key element in gathering the information upon which to base decisions. Therefore, instead of asking *What is it?*, *What does it do?*, and *What else does it do?*, ask *What should it be?*, *What should it do?*, and *What else should it do?* Even if you have arrived at a tentative definition, design, or other decision, use this process of analysis as an acid test.

Suppose you were to use this type of analysis in trying to decide what kind of consultant you ought to seek? The answer to *What should the consultant be?* is *Packaging consultant*. But now that you have an expanded, well-thought-out definition of packaging, you must come up with a more sophisticated and thoughtful answer than that. You must frame new questions, such as, *What is a packaging consultant?* or, perhaps more appropriately, *What should a packaging consultant be?* The latter question includes the tacit phrase *in this case* as an appendix to it. That is necessary because, as you have seen, *packaging* and *packaging consultant* are terms that have different meanings in different cases.

THE VALUE OF VALUE MANAGEMENT: A SUMMATION

Value management has an almost immediate application to many aspects of defining your needs and deciding what kind of consultant you need. Of course, you would have first identified a need or problem of some kind in general terms and then determined that you required some special help to satisfy the need or solve the problem. In general, the kinds of needs and problems that might lead you to seek consulting help most often fall into two broad categories: the need for special expertise that is not available as an in-house resource or the need for extra technical or professional help on a short-term basis. However, there are other reasons for seeking consulting help that, although they are less frequently encountered, are no less valid, and there are various situations in which the more common needs are encountered. To delineate these situations more clearly and help you recognize such situations when they arise in your own organization, consider the following examples.

1. You are temporarily shorthanded and need extra staff for some technical or professional functions. This may be because some of your own staff are ill, on vacation, or otherwise unavailable; because your workload is growing and

your personnel department is having difficulty hiring enough of the right people rapidly; because you have a temporary bulge in your workload; or other reasons. The point is that you need some technical and/or professional help to augment your regular staff on a less than permanent basis.

2. You encounter an unusual problem that is entirely beyond the capabilities of your regular staff employees. It could be a computer problem, a financing problem, a marketing problem, or any of many other special problems.
3. Your staff people know or believe they know how to cope with a problem that has arisen, but you believe that they are not sufficiently expert and so you want to hire a devil's advocate to get a more objective, outside opinion to compare with the ideas of the staff.
4. You have a special project that is so different from the usual work you do that you believe it ought to be compartmentalized and handled as something entirely divorced from the routine work of your organization and your regular staff.
5. You want to conduct an investigation and analysis, discuss the situation with an expert, and solicit an expert opinion and recommendation in a matter that is so sensitive or confidential that you do not wish your own staff to be aware of it.
6. You want an opinion from someone who is completely outside your organization—has not even been on your premises and has absolutely no prior knowledge of your organization and staff—so that you can be reasonably sure of a truly objective analysis, opinion, and recommendation, totally untainted by even indirect contact with your organization and staff.
7. You are trying to promote a plan or a change of some sort

to senior management in your organization, but they have resisted all arguments so far. You believe that they will give a great deal more credence to a study and presentation made by an outside consultant specialist. Or, as a variation on this, top management in your organization has authorized you to make a study to support or demolish your arguments, and it is necessary to have the study done by someone from the outside to avoid even the suspicion of bias.

8. You need more help, but for one reason or another (e.g., a hiring freeze or ceiling on staff levels) you are unable to hire anyone. However, you do have a budget from which you can hire consultants, and you can justify doing that. That would relieve your problem for a time—at least until the new budget year begins or the freeze is lifted.

All of these are situations confronting executives every day, and all are reasons to seek out a suitable consultant. But which consultant? How do you decide what kind of consultant you need? (You must decide that first, of course, before you can even think about where and how to find and choose the best consultant for your purposes.)

The first step in the process is one of identifying and defining the need or problem confronting you. That is not always the easiest thing to do, and it is quite easy to deceive yourself about just how difficult it is.

Chapter Four

Resources for Finding a Consultant

Despite the large number of consultants in practice, finding those most suitable for your needs is not always an easy task.

FINDING CONSULTANTS: INITIAL RESEARCH

There are consultants in almost every field of human endeavor, but when you seek a consultant to help you with a given need—especially if you have never before gone in quest of a consultant—you run into at least the following potential difficulties.

Technical and professional specialists do not always think of themselves as consultants and therefore are not listed as such, although what they do is, in fact, what most of us define as *consulting*. You may have to search for a "sales expert" or "marketing specialist" when you are seeking a sales consultant, for example.

Consultants often use other adjectives than you think of in describing their special fields of interest. For example, you may find a "meetings consultant" as suitable to your needs as a "travel consultant," but in your quest for one of these you may overlook "convention consultants, "convention managers," and others with related functional titles. To conduct an effective search, it is important to know all the terms by which a given kind or class of consultants, especially those who do not use the word *consultant*, identify themselves.

Many consultants use extremely broad terms such as *management consultant* that are not helpful when you are trying to find the specialist you need. Often you need to know more precise terms to identify what you seek. There are many titles by which consultants identify themselves. The appendix to this book describes many kinds of technical, business, and professional specialties, beyond the well-known ones such as lawyers, dentists, accountants, and physicians. Note, however, that many of the categories listed are quite broad and can be modified by many adjectives. "Appraisers," for example, includes real estate appraisers, gem appraisers, machinery appraisers, art appraisers, business appraisers, and many other kinds.

It may even be impossible to compile complete listings since new consulting specialties spring up continually as a result of new developments, but this is a start. (One relatively recent surge in the development of consulting specialties has been the huge growth in litigation in the United States. An entire field of consulting today is that of "expert witness," a specialist who is paid a consulting fee to appear in court to testify as an expert. Some specialties—environmental pollution, accident prevention, and labor legislation, for example—are represented in the appendix.)

Before examining these lists of *what* to look for, a few words about *where* to look should be helpful. The following checklist points up some preliminary steps to take before searching for specific categories of interest.

PLACES TO BEGIN LOOKING

1. Inquire among your friends and associates, seeking referrals and recommendations.
2. Seek out relevant professional, technical, or other associations and make inquiries there—that is, make your wants and needs known. (See the lists in the appendix.)
3. Inquire of and—make your wants and business opportunities known to editors of publications read by consultants. (See the lists in the appendix.)
4. Use paid advertising to solicit interest, perhaps announcing the availability of a request for proposals or some other opportunity for readers to pursue the business opportunity.
5. Subscribe to or register with one of the several network or directory services designed especially for the purpose of helping clients and consultants find each other.
6. Check on the books and journals of the relevant fields.

Consultants and other specialists often write books and articles, partly to help make themselves known to prospective clients. Your librarian can help you find printed guides to books, magazines, and specific articles, all of which are cataloged.

7. Check the telephone Yellow Pages. Consultants are rarely listed under "Consultants," but are usually under the relevant technical or professional specialty (e.g., "Engineers—Consulting").
8. Pay attention to your own morning mail. Even so-called junk mail often contains valuable clues and leads.
9. Collect and keep on file relevant business cards, brochures, and capabilities statements for reference.

USING PERIODICALS

There are three ways to use periodicals in your quest. One is to run paid advertising in them. Even inexpensive classified advertising will draw enthusiastic response if placed in the right periodicals—those read by consultants. However, not all periodicals, especially newsletters, accept paid advertising, and even those that do accept it often do not accept classified advertising. On the other hand, publishers of business and professional periodicals are usually delighted to tell their readers about sales opportunities, and a news release or even a letter to the editor will often bring you editorial coverage and enthusiastic response from readers. Finally, *read* relevant journals, seeking mention of consultants and writing by consultants.

All of these approaches are likely to produce a list of candidates, of whom it is likely that only a few are likely to prove to be right for you. These methods will probably produce an abundance of applicants for the contract, thereby presenting you with the problem of determining who is right for your needs. Doing this screening to make a choice is often the most difficult and time-consuming task in the entire process, but it is an absolute necessity.

SCREENING THE LIST

If the project is small and the number of candidate consultants is also small, screening may consist simply of conducting individual interviews and selecting the individual who makes the best impression in the interview. For small projects, more elaborate (and thus more costly) screening is not justified. With larger projects—which means larger budgets and greater risk—greater numbers of candidate consultants appear and more efficient screening methods are required. Direct interviews of all would be time-consuming, difficult, and expensive, prohibitively so. Screening must ordinarily be done by stages, with a first, rough screen to eliminate the obviously unsuited candidates and often a second, intermediate screen to filter out the remaining few candidates for final selection.

It is for this reason that governments and other large organizations turn to formal procurement procedures that are based on well-organized search, screening, and contract-award processes. Typically, they include the following steps and phases:

1. Publishing a synopsis of the requirement (e.g., general service to be provided or problem to be solved) in some suitable medium, inviting interested and qualified candidates to compete.
2. Mailing out a solicitation package consisting of a statement of work, description of response required (bid, quotation, or proposal), and supporting information and documents.

3. Reviewing and evaluating contenders on the basis of their qualifications and the merit of their offers, as exhibited by their responses (proposals/bids).
4. Meeting with one or more of the top contenders for discussions, so-called best and final offers, and/or direct negotiation.
5. Making the final decision and contract award.

GATHERING CAPABILITIES STATEMENTS

For those who use consulting services more than occasionally and for those who have a sizeable contract to award and so are planning the procurement many months in advance, there is an excellent resource available to aid in researching the field of suitable candidates for the project. That is the gathering up of *capabilities statements* from all interested candidates. Executives in federal government agencies do this quite often when a long-range program is planned or the agency has frequent need of expert help. The federal agency planning the program will make an announcement in the government's official daily periodical, the *Commerce Business Daily*, explaining the program and contemplated need in broad terms and inviting interested readers to submit capabilities statements that explain their qualifications to contract for work on the program. The announcement usually specifies that only those who have submitted such capabilities statements and have been judged qualified will be permitted to compete for participation in the program. Later, when the client agency is ready, solicitation packages are sent out inviting proposals.

Paid advertisements soliciting capabilities statements will produce an abundance of these. But it is not always necessary to use paid advertising; most newsletters and journals read by technical and professional experts are pleased to run such announcements in their editorial matter as a service to their readers.

JUST WHAT IS A CAPABILITIES STATEMENT?

Not everyone is familiar with the term *capabilities statement* (also sometimes referred to as a *capabilities brochure*), so it is not amiss to furnish a brief explanation of that document here. This explanation is based on both the philosophical or applications definition and the physical description.

The Philosophical/Applications Definition

A capabilities statement is often compared with a proposal, possibly because many people prepare capabilities statements in physical formats that resemble proposals and possibly because those familiar with proposals tend to see the capabilities statement as a kind of generalized proposal. The comparison is an unrealistic one for several reasons, but principally because the proposal is a sales presentation, designed to sell a specific project or program that is proposed, usually in response to a perceived problem that the client has. The capabilities statement, on the other hand, is a form of general advertising intended primarily to describe the author's field and establish credentials or acceptability for future sales presentations. It is designed to generate leads for sales, and you should regard it in that light.

From another viewpoint, a capabilities statement is a specialized calling card. Its purpose is primarily to acquaint a prospective client with the qualifications of the consultant or consultant firm and the author's suitability as a candidate for assignments and contracts. It is not expected that anyone writing a capabilities statement will be awarded a contract as a direct result of that statement; rather, it is expected that the statement will encourage the prospective client to invite bids, quotations, and/or proposals from its author. The consultant submitting such a statement does not expect any other result, and so the capabilities statement should be reviewed in that light. It is merely introductory, intended to establish the author's qualifications as a consultant expert and/or a qualified and competent service, willing and able to plan and provide solutions to clients' problems.

No capabilities statement ought to attempt more than this, and no client should read more than this into the statement.

The Physical Definition/Description

Physically, a capabilities statement is a brochure or letter that explains what the issuing organization or individual consultant can do. It may be lengthy or short, depending on circumstances, and it can be relatively informal. If the consultant is restricted to some highly standardized service or set of services—possibly even proprietary services or those based on some proprietary item—the statement is likely to be a formally typeset capabilities brochure, printed and distributed freely and in large quantities. But consultants who normally deliver custom-designed services or sets of services to clients are more likely to offer a capabilities statement typed up individually as a response to a request for capabilities brochures or as a follow-up to a marketing visit.

Those who hire consultants frequently and/or who have planned for a long time to hire one or more consultants for a large project (e.g., federal government agencies) often collect capabilities brochures in preparation for inviting proposals, using them as a basic bidders' mailing list. Some even announce their contemplated project many months ahead, explaining it in broad terms and inviting prospective competitors to qualify as bidders or proposers by submitting acceptable capabilities brochures, as many federal agencies do.

Content: What Should You Expect to See?

Typically, the capabilities statement describes the consultant in terms of experience and accomplishments, lists relevant resources, and explains the services offered. In general, the content will include the following:

1. Type(s) of services offered
2. Some typical clients, both listed generically and identified by name
3. Resumé(s) of principal practitioner(s)
4. Listing and description of general facilities and other resources
5. Special notes such as the following (may be appended or may be incorporated in resumés or elsewhere):

   Patents awarded

   Papers published

   Special facilities/resources

   Special/noteworthy achievements

   Honors and awards

   Details (at least noteworthy ones) of recent projects

HOW SHOULD YOU EVALUATE A CAPABILITIES STATEMENT?

There is something of an anomaly involved in answering the question of what a capabilities statement is. By its nature, a capabilities statement must be generalized, since it is largely exploratory—almost a substitute for a calling card, as noted earlier—and responds to either a most general description of future need or to only an undefined and general prospect of possible need. In some respects, the evaluation of a capabilities statement parallels that of a proposal (discussed later), but there are significant differences too.

Consciously or unconsciously, you are influenced both favorably and unfavorably by certain factors in such a statement. It is helpful to become conscious of those factors so you can be alert to them and recognize them.

The Matter of Specifics

The least effective advertising is that which is sometimes characterized as "Madison Avenue," relying heavily on inflated claims supported by nothing more substantial than assorted superlatives. Such writing is characteristically heavily larded with *largest, greatest, most advanced,* and other such self-congratulatory adjectives and adverbs. For the discriminating reader such terms have an adverse effect, the opposite of the one sought: The more they appear, the less credible the presentation is. And that is as it should be. The late Bertrand Russell, noted physicist, mathematician, and philosopher, remarked that one appeals to faith when there is no evidence to support a contention. Likewise, it might be said that one resorts to hyperbole when one has no facts to support a contention. That is the effect that hyperbole has: It suggests that the author has no useful facts to offer. And that is the conclusion a reader ought to draw from such a presentation.

Even beyond that, it is difficult to accept claims of competence—much less of excellence—when the claim is made in a statement that is all generalization, without specific detail of any kind. In judging the value of a capabilities statement, it is important to weigh the degree to which the statement offers specific *facts,* as contrasted with vague claims of any kind. Skillful writing may lend a general impression of specificity when there is really none, so it is necessary to study the presentation with a conscious quest for specificity.

The Matter of Detail

Closely related to specificity is the matter of detail. True, the capabilities statement is a generalized one in that it does not address a specific client's need to be met or problem to be solved. It should, nevertheless, present the details of the items listed earlier as typical of the information to be expected in a capabilities statement. The more detail it includes, the more credible it is to the discriminating reader. Since almost anyone can generalize about almost any subject, generalities do not prove the author's credentials. The presence of abundant detail has the opposite effect: It tends to demonstrate that the author is indeed expert and is well informed in discussing the types of problems and services to be provided. Beyond that, the willingness of the author to make the commitment to a detailed description and discussion speaks eloquently of the proposer's confidence in what he or she has to offer. It is therefore extremely helpful to be alert to whether the capabilities statement is truly specific and offers an ample array of details in what it presents or whether it is an effort to persuade and convince with glib generalities—what is, in the argot, a "snow job."

One executive of a large organization remarked that while he sympathized with and tried to offer as much as he could to small businesses, he was always disenchanted immediately by what was to him a readily apparent snow job: hyperbole and pompous, inflated language—especially when used incorrectly—and a lengthy company name that was obviously intended to impress. As this executive put it, "The smaller the company the bigger the name."

There is a great deal to be said for simple honesty. As a prospective client, you cannot help but have misgivings about doing business with someone who is patently less than honest in his or her literature, especially in a capabilities statement. There is certainly no stigma attached to being a small business. In fact it can often be advantageous in several ways to do business with small organizations and even independent consultants, especially those with enough integrity and confidence in themselves to be completely honest in their representations to prospective clients. An important criterion of quality in a capabilities statement is, therefore, the basic honesty—or lack of it—that inevitably manages to appear between the lines of text, no matter how fluent the writing.

The Matter of Relevance

There are always contenders for contracts who are not really well qualified—that is, they may be well qualified for some other requirement but are not well qualified to satisfy your need, *even if they do provide specific details.* It is not unprecedented for clients reviewing capabilities statements to be blinded by glib writing and ample details and thus fail to perceive that the qualifications presented are not truly relevant to the need.

A capabilities statement is not a resumé, although a resumé is a part of the statement and usually a key element. However, the same evaluation criteria and standards may be applied: general qualifications, specific qualifications, and relevant accomplishments. General qualifications center primarily on formal education and training, and specific qualifications center on relevant experience and resources such as facilities. The record and presentation of relevant accomplishments is quite another matter. It should answer the question "What have you done that benefited earlier clients or employers?" as an indication of more-than-ordinary capabilities.

The Question of Achievements

If you have an ordinary competitive spirit you will not and should not be satisfied with routine skills and abilities, the kind that *any* consultant would probably be able to offer and the kind that are available to your competitors. You want more, a service above the ordinary. So the most basic question in your mind as you study each capabilities statement ought to be "What can you—will you—do for me?" It is only by reviewing the contender's earlier achievements that you can infer an answer to that question. It is in that connection that some of those items listed as "special notes"—patents, special facilities and resources, and special achievements—begin to assume their proper significance.

Degrees of Competence

People tend to assume, as an article of faith, that everyone who prepares and files a statement of capabilities is a fully competent practitioner of whatever craft or professional field is of concern. Many tend to fall into the trap of believing in competence as an absolute quality that either does or does not exist in each given case and that is so absolute that each competent practitioner is the equal of every other.

That is not so, of course. There are many degrees of competence between the extremes of outstanding performers and incompetent performers. Any individual may be anywhere along that spectrum of best to worst.

For practical purposes it is necessary to separate the individuals—your judgment of the available candidates—into groups of competent, incompetent, and semicompetent contenders. It is that last type that represents the problem. It is relatively easy to recognize and identify those at the extremes, but the semicompetents are glib, have some familiarity with the field, and are often so convincing that they convince themselves. They truly do not understand their own shortcomings.

These types are encountered everywhere—as automobile mechanics, as physicians, as bureaucrats, as lawyers, as accountants, and as managers of various kinds. They are dangerous because they are convincing and probably are sincere, unaware of their deficiencies in technical or professional abilities.

It is important to be well aware of this special hazard and be both alert to and able to recognize the breed. One clue to this has been covered already: the lack of ability to provide specific detail. However, that is not always enough, for you must evaluate the detail that is provided as to its sensibility and accuracy.

References and Credentials

One of the most important credentials is recommendations by others and/or their verifications of the representations you read in the capabilities statements of contenders. Capabilities statements often carry lengthy lists of current and former clients, sometimes with the names of individuals who can verify the author's claims.

It is not always practical to ask the authors of capabilities statements to provide such details when they have not done so of their own volition, but it is advisable to note the lack of such information and to ask for it later, in the request for proposals.

The Most Critical Consideration

The essence of the successful proposal in the competition for contracts is not proof that "I can do it too" or "I can do it as well as the next guy." The ability to "do it as well as the next guy" is taken for granted; the automatic assumption (not always justified, but nevertheless a normal assumption) is that each competitor is basically qualified. But that does not and certainly should not win contracts, because being "as good as the next guy" is not nearly enough. The contract usually goes to the consultant who is better than the others—the one who demonstrates the unusual, more innovative, more highly qualified, more imaginative, more effective, or otherwise superior capability. That is the essence of success for the consultant, and it should be the major criterion of and selection for you as the client.

It is not usually too difficult to recognize and identify the unquestionably competent, and the unquestionably incompetent but it is often quite difficult to recognize those individuals whose major talent appears to lie in reflecting an aura of competence because they have some basic knowledge of the field and are glib, but who are not really able. Demonstration of superior qualifications ought to be a major factor in the capabilities statement, too. True enough, everyone who shows basic capability is ethically entitled to compete for the contract, but it is certainly in your own interest, as the potential client, to note the unusually well-qualified contender when you study capabilities statements. Doing so alerts you to facts that will be valuable when you make decisions later on.

For example, it may be that you will have far too many capabilities statements—too many contenders for the contract—and will want to winnow them to some more manageable number. There is a practical limit to how many proposals you can study and evaluate, and this is a major criterion for screening out the less promising applicants. It is in your interest to encourage submittal of a maximum number of capabilities statements and then do this kind of screening and winnowing. This process produces the best crop of proposals, which is the next topic of discussion.

Chapter Five

Soliciting Bids and Proposals

What has gone before is prologue, important information about choosing and using consultants but leading up to what experience suggests is the most critical element of the process: both inducing consultants to submit worthy proposals and enabling them to do so.

ARE PROPOSALS IMPORTANT?

Consultants do not use proposals enough; that is, they rarely use them unless a client requests them. But clients do not request then often enough, either. When the client wants a consultant specialist to carry out a large and complex project, the client usually develops a request for proposals. However, when the task is relatively small (e.g., staff augmentation for a few days or assistance in writing a small report), the client tends to avoid going to the trouble of requesting proposals.

In both cases, this is probably largely due to reluctance to undertake writing tasks. Many professionals, highly educated and highly talented, intensely dislike writing. Clients who require small-scale consulting services therefore often tend to rely on personal resumés, brochures, and direct interviews for selecting consultants.

That is a mistake. First of all, requesting proposals for a small project does not entail a major writing chore. Informal or letter proposals serve admirably when the task is a small one. Moreover, once you have written your first request for proposals, you have a model that is the basis for future ones, and each request after that becomes easier to write.

Bear in mind, then, in the discussions to follow, that while requests and proposals are often large documents, they are also often little more than letters, and these discussions apply to both kinds of documents.

A CONSULTANT'S VIEW

Jeffrey Geibel, an independent management consultant in the Boston area, sums up the need for a proposal as follows:

> The need for proposals in consulting is established in part by

the fact that consultants are usually providing an intangible (advice or expertise), and communication is critical in the marketing of an intangible.

He goes on to point to the need for understanding between client and consultant, making it clear that *understanding* and *communication* are interchangeable terms in this context, and he cites a number of specific reasons to support the idea that proposals are necessary:

1. People forget.
2. People make mistakes.
3. People leave their jobs after making commitments.
4. People tend to hear what they want to hear.
5. Some people will try to take advantage of any "misunderstandings."
6. In general, things change.
7. Proposals provide a documented record.

The document from which these items are quoted is one that offers the reader a great deal of guidance in and observations about proposal writing. It also views the need for proposals from the consultant's standpoint. If you reread these brief passages you may perceive that there is no way of knowing whether they were addressed to the client or to the consultant: The points made are as relevant to the interests of one as they are to the other.

There is a simple but important truth to be deduced here: Proposals are equally useful to both client and consultant. In general, for the consultant, proposals represent sales opportunities; for the client, they represent an excellent means of evaluating candidates for the work required. However, there are other considerations, some that are especially important to the consultant and others that are especially important to the client. The ones that are especially important to the client will be explored here.

BENEFITS TO YOU AS A CLIENT

From your viewpoint as a client, there are a number of reasons for requesting proposals. The overall reason, as already noted, is the use of the proposal as an important aid in choosing a consultant. But there are other reasons, at least one of which is often equally important if your request for proposals includes an adequate statement of work. It is this: Proposals often provide valuable technical information, are helpfully diagnostic in nature, and shed light on new aspects of your problem or need that, despite your own best efforts, you had not perceived. You will find, if you request proposals very often, that many proposers show surprisingly astute insight into your needs; they often help you gain a better understanding of your needs than you had when you wrote the request!

There are some consultants who fear that clients interviewing them are deliberately trying to pick their brains—to get something for nothing. They sometimes offer advice to other consultants on how to avoid giving away their stock in trade. This fear, and some antidotes to it, will be discussed later. However, it would disturb me greatly, as a client, to be regarded with such suspicion, and it would make me apprehensive about doing business with a person exhibiting such fears, whether in face-to-face discussions or in proposal responses. I would think carefully about the possibility that such an individual might not be entirely frank and forthcoming with me even when I was paying for the services.

A BUILT-IN DILEMMA

This is not to say that you should use requests for proposals (hereafter referred to also as *RFPs*) for the cynical purpose of "picking the brains" of consultants. Far from it. Requesting proposals for such a dishonest purpose is a reprehensible practice that, I am happy to report, occurs rather infrequently, and then almost always as the unauthorized and unscrupulous actions of an irresponsible maverick in the organization and not as an organization-approved procedure. Still, if you have done your homework—made a careful analysis and included in your RFP a carefully detailed, complete, and accurate statement of work as you see it together with a well-thought-out specification of the response required—you will usually be rewarded with a wealth of valuable technical information provided by the proposal writers as an inevitable result of the normal processes involved in soliciting and receiving proposals.

This result is inevitable because the end goal of soliciting proposals is to gain a basis for evaluating not only the consultants qualifications, but also their understanding of your need and the virtues of what they propose to do about satisfying the need. If you do not get proposals that furnish information suitable for these evaluations, it is futile to even request the proposals. Thus it is essential that in your RFP you specifically ask for and get enough detailed information on which to base your judgment. The subject of what ought to be included in your RFP will be discussed later.

THE OTHER SIDE OF THE COIN

Important as the proposal is, and despite the benefits it offers you as a client, there are drawbacks: The entire business of soliciting and using proposals to choose consultants is a time-consuming and expensive one. You have the time spent in writing the RFP plus the costs of carrying out some, possibly all, of the following procedures:

1. Developing the solicitation package—the RFP and all the elements required to make up the package.
2. Compiling a list of prospects—consultants who will be invited to submit proposals.
3. Reading, reviewing, evaluating the proposals submitted.
4. Holding "best-and-final" conferences with some or all proposers to get clarifications, discuss critical points raised, and ask for amendments to or revisions of proposals.
5. Negotiating contract(s).

None of these steps is a simple one, as will become evident in the discussion of what is involved in each of them. It is thus small wonder that clients tend to favor alternative methods and sometimes turn to requiring proposals somewhat reluctantly and only as a last resort.

ALTERNATIVES TO PROPOSALS

The leading alternative to the proposal is the bid. The nominal advantage of soliciting bids, rather than proposals, is that the entire procurement and contracting process is simplified: The evaluation is now simply a matter of determining who, among those bidding and apparently qualified, is the low bidder. He or she is the winner. Unfortunately, it is not always quite that simple.

In government procurement, for example, the bid is, first of all, open to everyone who wishes to compete, and so it must be *advertised* (the term has a rather special meaning in this context), and bids must be accepted from anyone and everyone. Bids are usually sealed by statutory requirement. That is, they are kept secret until the deadline, at which time no further bids are accepted and the bids are unsealed publicly and read aloud to all who choose to be present at their opening. (These are usually the bidders themselves, not surprisingly.) Usually, only failure to sign a bid or supply some specific information requested, or having been previously barred from bidding because of some offense, will disqualify a bidder. This is the exception, however, far more than it is the rule.

The client in the private-sector organization is usually under no such constraints unless the organization's policy and procedures mandate it or there are other exceptions such as those noted earlier. However, the net result is usually the same: The low bidder wins the contract. But there is one difference: In government procurement practices, because of statutory controls, it is all but inevitable that the low bidder will win the contract unless there is a powerful reason to disqualify that bidder (a relatively rare event). This has led distressingly often to unhappy government agencies reluctantly awarding contracts to low bidders who appear unsuitable and who, all too often, prove to be just that—unqualified and unable to perform satisfactorily. On the other hand, private-sector clients are under no such statutory restraints and so may opt to ignore the low bidder for any reason at all and choose another bidder at their own pleasure.

It is important to understand this distinction. Obviously, you must understand your own organization's policies and, if germane, and legal requirements that affect your handling of bids. (For example, if you are the recipient of grants or other public funds, you may be subject to statutory controls similar to those that affect the government's own procurements, and you must also be alert to civil rights laws that may affect you decisions.) But it is also important that you anticipate understandings and misunderstandings on the part of bidders. For example, if you are a client in a private-sector organization and under no compulsion to accept the low bid simply because it *is* a low bid, it is probably wise to make this absolutely clear in your solicitation package. Failure to do so may lead to marked unpleasantness with the low bidder if you choose to disqualify the low bidder or choose another for any reason.

Why Are Low Bids Often Unacceptable?

Business conditions and competitive efforts sometimes lead to illogical situations, and competitive bids offer many examples. Business organizations in uncomfortable straits or new ones struggling to get started will often undertake desperate measures such as bidding for work they do not understand well and are not well qualified to handle. In situations in which there are no tight restrictions on who is permitted to bid, there are frequently bidders who quote figures in both unrealistically high and unrealistically low ranges. For example, in one situation in which the realistic range was $16,000 to $20,000, the low bid was about $5,000 and the high bid was over $80,000. It was clear that these bidders were making desperate (and wild) guesses and had no real understanding of what was required. A government agency usually has no choice but to accept the low bid unless it can find grounds for disqualification or persuade the bidder to voluntarily withdraw the bid. That is the downside of statutory control of procurement. It is also the reason government agencies often tend to prefer the proposal route, despite its problems: They are not compelled to accept the low bidder when using competitive proposals—negotiated procurement—but can exercise their judgment in deciding what is in the government's best interest.

Aside from the mandate of statutory requirement, there are more subtle pressures to accept the low bid, even when the bid is so unrealistically low as to create doubts about the bidder's grasp of the problem and capability for solving it and you are not truly obligated to accept the low bid. For one thing, there is the natural instinct to take advantage of every bargain opportunity. But a more powerful force is the fear that you will be unable to justify rejecting the low bid, should your decision be challenged, and especially should the low bidder, having lost, appeal to higher-level management in the organization.

Aside from this, the traditional bidding system, whether sealed or not, does not normally afford much of an opportunity to evaluate each bidder's professional abilities: Bids normally require from the bidder only a set of numbers—costs or prices and terms—although you might receive or already have in your possession a copy of the bidder's capability statement and other pertinent literature. Even that is far less substance upon which to base a decision than a full-blown proposal.

The drawbacks just cited are among the reasons that even in the private sector many clients prefer to avoid the traditional sealed-bid procurement process.

A Middle-of-the-Road Alternative

The bid is not the only alternative to the proposal. There is at least one other common approach taken: You issue a request for quotations and select one for award or for negotiation.

One major difference between a bid and a quotation, under normal circumstances at least, is that a bid once submitted is binding on the bidder, whereas a quotation is not binding on either party. The government client will often issue a request for quotation (RFQ) only to those who are considered well qualified, often requesting a capabilities statement with the quotation. Having chosen one bidder, the agency will call to verify the quotation and the bidder's willingness to accept an order. Confirming that, the agency will usually issue a purchase order as the contractual instrument, although some agencies prefer to issue a more formal contract instrument.

Requesting quotations enables you to avoid the burden of being pressured or forced to accept a low bid, on the one hand, while it also avoids the great expense in dollars and time required to solicit proposals; thus, it is a middle-of-the-road or compromise solution.

When to Use Each Alternative

It should not be assumed from this that deciding what means to turn to in choosing and contracting with a consultant is a matter of whim or purely arbitrary. There are definite reasons for each choice. The matter of why and when the bid procedure is justified will be examined first. Bear in mind here that the bid procedure gives you the least control of the award and the least information upon which to base a final decision.

The Logic—and Illogic—of the Bid Procedure

Logically, the use of competitive bids should be chosen only under one of two sets of conditions:

1. When all candidates are considered to be so equal to each other in all respects that the only significant difference is cost.
2. When the product or service required can be specified so precisely and accurately that the only difference between or among what can be delivered (i.e., what you will accept) is cost.

The sealed bid is the most efficient means of purchasing, in many ways, but it is also the most hazardous when your situation is less well defined than the situations described here. It can be a most illogical choice in that case.

Small Purchases Generally

Unfortunately, some clients are misled into opting for bids under a third condition that they believe justifies—perhaps even mandates—a bid procedure as the initial step in procurement. That is sometimes the case when the purchase is a relatively small one, so that the client believes it improvident and perhaps even inefficient to go to the expense of getting proposals written. But that is a mistake, because there are ways of using the proposal process most economically, without sacrificing its benefits, when the purchase is a small one. That will be discussed shortly. For now, it is useful to look at some other ways of making small purchases when the budget and/or nature of the need makes the use of small-purchase procedures appear to be the most sensible one.

The Logic of the Request for Quotations

In government agencies, issuing a request for quotations as the first step in a procurement is normally done only when the purchase qualifies under the authority of small-purchases laws and the service or product required either can be specified in detail or is rather ordinary and does not require particularly specialized skills or problem solving. In the federal government, under current law, small purchases are those under $25,000; in state and local government, the limit is somewhat lower and varies from one jurisdiction to another. In private-sector organizations, of course, the limit is a matter of internal policy, usually set by formal procedures in large organizations and by individual judgment of an authorizing executive in smaller ones.

A Hybrid Method as a Compromise

There is one other method of procurement, a method that combines the best features of sealed bids and competitive proposals.

It is known as a *two-step procurement*, and it works in this manner:

1. Technical proposals without cost estimates are requested.
2. The proposals are evaluated and judged acceptable or not acceptable.
3. Authors of proposals judged acceptable are invited to submit cost estimates.
4. The low bidder is awarded the contract.

The basis of this method is that it provides control of bidders by prequalifying—or disqualifying—them. The advantages are obvious. The disadvantage is the difficulty of drawing the line between qualification and disqualification and the danger of exposing yourself to a possible obligation to award the contract to the least qualified of those whose proposals were acceptable.

More Informal Uses of Small-Purchase Authority

Actually, the issuance of a formal request for quotations is not an absolute necessity, but is largely a matter of convenience in getting quotations and finding the lowest-cost sources, as well as a convenient means for establishing a good paper trail—a formal record of transactions and accountability. Quotations can also be requested by ordinary correspondence (letters of inquiry) or even verbally, in some cases, and there are other means for establishing complete records of transactions. In most systems, federal and other, the point is not so much the specific methodology used as it is compliance with the philosophies of competitive bidding and small-purchase authority. That compliance can be satisfied in several ways, of which the formal request for quotations is only one.

INFORMAL OR LETTER PROPOSALS

A few years ago I sauntered into the downtown Washington, D.C., offices of the Occupational Safety and Health Administration (OSHA), an agency within the U.S. Department of Labor. After talking with a number of people, I found myself opposite an executive of the agency's training office. We communicated well with each other: I inquired into his problems and was able to arouse his interest in the solution I proposed to his most pressing problem of the moment. (Unlike many of my contemporaries, I did not fear having my "brains picked.") He invited me to submit to him an informal and unsolicited proposal—a *letter proposal*—describing in writing what I had proposed verbally, with my estimated cost.

I did so, asking for $2,400 for my proposed effort (the statutory small-purchase limit was then $2,500), and was rewarded with a purchase order in that amount. The point is that this is not an unusual procurement process. On the contrary, it is quite ordinary, and you can often find and retain capable consultants in just this manner. Since the request was made verbally by my client in a face-to face discussion, he did not have to go to the trouble of writing anything at that point. Later, after receiving and accepting my letter proposal, he had to write only a request for issuance of a purchase order, and he used a few sentences from my proposal to describe what the purchase order was for! It was a convenient method for both of us.

Informal (Letter) Proposals Versus Formal Proposals

The difference between formal and informal, or letter, proposals is far more a matter of size than it is of kind. In fact, it should be understood clearly that the use of the adjective *informal,* when applied to a letter proposal, refers only to the lack of the niceties of formal publications usually found in the full-blown or formal proposal: cover, title page, table of contents, figures, and other such costly refinements. The lack of such publication formalities is relatively insignificant; it reflects only the sensible refusal to risk hundreds or even thousands of dollars in pursuit of a small contract. Nor would the thoughtful client expect a consultant to be so profligate; in fact, it would reflect an alarming lack of cost consciousness and, therefore, a lack of prudence, not a laudable characteristic nor one that might endear a consultant to a prospective client.

THE ELEMENTS OF A PROPOSAL

In both kinds of proposals, formal and informal, the basic elements are the same, for you need the same kind of information to hire a consultant for a small project as you do to hire one for a large project. At a minimum, proposals should include the following kinds of information:

1. Introduction of the author—who he or she is, by name and generically, and why the proposal is offered—with a statement of intent (e.g., to respond to a stated need or request by the client or to offer some specific service or product).

   This should include a clear and concise identification, understanding, and/or appraisal of your need or problem delivered in terms that demonstrate that the consultant does understand it. (Distressingly often, clients get proposals that make the author appear to be knocking on the wrong door, with no understanding of the need or problem.)

2. A discussion of the need, including analysis and rationale, in enough detail to demonstrate that the consultant has the

necessary understanding, skills, and plan for approaching and satisfying the need. This should end with a clearly defined approach.

3. A clear and specific description of the effort proposed: how the approach described will be implemented, with a detailed explanation of the program and what the consultant proposes to do, step by step. This should include a description of any and all items to be delivered to the client with schedule dates to be met.
4. The technical/professional qualifications of the consultant: formal education and training; experience; accounts of other, similar projects; facilities and resources, as relevant; references; and other relevant information.

Included with or appended to this information, as appropriate, may be drawings, charts, and/or other exhibits.

THE SOLICITATION PACKAGE

Evaluating proposals is not a simple task. Of course, it is not the proposal per se that you are trying to evaluate, but the proposer and the plans presented by the proposer. You are, in fact, trying to choose the right consultant and right plan or approach for your need. (And I emphasize the use of the word *right,* rather than *best* here.) You are trying to qualify each response to your RFP to find the best match with your needs. You are seeking certain factors in the responses. You are looking for the response that best demonstrates that the proposer

- understands your requirement clearly;
- offers a plan that makes sense and appears most likely to do the job successfully;

- has the right qualifications to execute the plan successfully;
- and is a reliable contractor.

Information You Should Supply

Even when you understand the broad requirement to qualify proposers on all counts enumerated here, it is still difficult to set absolute standards as a basis for evaluating them. That forces you to perform much of the evaluation on a comparative or competitive basis, trying to select the best of the lot. One difficulty that is often encountered, even if you have worked hard to develop a few standards for evaluation, is that the proposals are so dissimilar that it is difficult to compare them with each other or to measure them against any standards you have developed.

That leads to the notion that you should require proposers to follow certain guidelines—that you should dictate content and format, at least within broad limits. That, in fact, is what organizations who hire many consultants normally do. However, there is a caveat: You are in quest of custom services, normally, and often want the advantage of the consultant's analysis and ideas. So it is important to encourage proposers to offer their ideas freely by keeping the requested format somewhat flexible, while still ensuring some degree of uniformity in the final product. There is probably no single format that would fit all cases, nor is it desirable to restrict yourself to any single format. However, it is possible to suggest a general format that should achieve the proper balance and yet be readily adaptable to a variety of needs and circumstances. Such a format will be suggested later. It is possible to influence the responses by the nature of the information you supply in your solicitation package. The following is the kind of information you should normally supply:

1. Identify and describe the problem or need that must be

solved or satisfied—the requirement—as accurately as possible, to wit:

a. If it is a problem to be solved, describe the symptoms—*all* the symptoms as you know them—*quantifying,* as well as *qualifying* them to the best of your ability. (The more information you provide here, the better the recommendations and proposed program you will get.)

b. Explain as accurately and adequately as you can the end result or end product you want (e.g., computer tape, manual, report, system design, drawings, etc.).

2. Specify the information you want to read in the proposal, keeping in mind what you need to make a sensible judgment and what the average consultant is likely to be able to provide within the confines of a proposal. But do ask for the following:

a. Evidence that the proposer fully understands your requirement (need or problem and end result or end product).

b. Information explaining the proposer's approach to satisfying the requirement, with arguments establishing the rationale for the approach and reasons for predicting success.

c. The specifics of the proposed program of work (who, what, when, where, etc.) including quantitative and qualitative data on end products and/or end results predicted and/or promised.

d. Full details of the proposer's qualifications for the work.

3. Specify your requirements concerning contracts, invoices, payments, and other pertinent legal and administrative details.

The Elements of the Package

The term *package* is not used here literally; it may refer to a thick bundle of documents if the procurement is a large one, or it may be a simple one- or two-page letter. It is just like the case of the formal proposal versus the informal or letter proposal: The elements are the same; only the scale is different. The elements are normally as follows:

1. An introductory statement briefly explaining the need and desired response and identifying the organization and name(s) of individual(s) in the organization that the proposer ought to know for responding, asking questions, or other follow-up. If it is likely that there will be questions (e.g., if the requirement is a complex one or has many uncertainty factors), explain the procedure the proposer is to follow in seeking additional information. This is a good place to stipulate the type of contract contemplated or to request that the proposer suggest one.
2. A statement of work, providing the detailed information concerning the requirement.
3. A detailed explanation of the information required in the response. Here, explain the desired format, if any special format is required, and any information you can or are willing to provide to explain the procedure by which you will evaluate responses and choose an awardee.
4. Any special information, such as your own organization's regulations or procedures for contracting out, a specimen contract, and other such details.

BID PACKAGES

So far, the discussion has focused on packages soliciting proposals, which is the type of solicitation you are most likely to want to use in retaining consultants. That is simply because the work is custom work and calls for a unique approach. Success depends on the factors listed earlier: the quality of the plan and the consultant's capabilities and dependability for executing the plan successfully. But there are circumstances under which you may feel justified in using the far more efficient procurement procedures under which competitive bids are solicited.

The most important single factor that determines whether you must turn to proposals or can use the more efficient competitive-bid method of procurement is whether difference in cost is the principal difference among a number of offers, as in the case of buying common commodities or goods and services that can be specified in detail. Despite the fact that, by the very nature of the work, ideas, capabilities, and approaches are usually the critical factors and therefore demand a proposal competition, there are exceptions. For example, suppose that you have a payroll program that require four hours to run and you have determined that it is possible to tighten the program or to write another program that will do the job in one hour. It is possible that you could prepare a specification that would be tight enough to enable you to award the contract on the basis of price alone. (The contract would include some test criteria that would enable you to verify complete conformance with your specification.)

In fact, when purchasing by competitive bids, it is as much in the bidder's interest as it is in your own to specify not only the product or service but also the means for verifying complete conformance. It minimizes the probability of serious contract disputes, which is also in your mutual interest. Thus, in considering whether sealed, competitive bidding, with contact award to the low bidder, is a viable choice, you must determine whether you can draw up these two specifications with sufficient precision. However, there is at least one alternative in which you can build in an escape hatch. That will be discussed in a moment.

The elements of the solicitation for bids are similar in most respects to those of the RFP, with the exception of directions for writing a proposal. Instead, the respondent should be helped to understand that the bid, unlike the quotation, represents a commitment by the bidder. In the government procurement system, the bidder is actually signing a contract in certifying and signing the bid, and the document cautions the bidder to therefore double-check and be certain of full understanding of both the requirement and the figures furnished. It is a wise idea to include this admonition in all bid solicitations.

Alternative Bid Forms

The greater efficiency—lower cost, less labor, and shorter time—is not the only advantage of the sealed bid over the proposal method of purchasing. In some respects, the sealed bid offers greater flexibility in contracting and in managing the work done under contract. Here is why.

Not all procurements made via competitive sealed bids are classic, straightforward, fixed-price agreements. There are variations, chief of which is the *indefinite-quantity* kind. If is often the case, especially in buying consulting services, that you know precisely what you want but either do not know how much of it you want or want to be able to make changes easily. This is generally accomplished by unitizing the work or the product and pricing accordingly. For example, suppose you want a professional temporary—perhaps a technical illustrator—to work on a program. Typically, you would price this service by some unit of time, using an hourly or a day rate. The bid would call for stipulating a rate, without firm commitment by the client as to total hours, although many clients would estimate quantity and some would even stipulate a minimum and maximum. Anything can be priced by units. For example, editorial work done on contract is sometimes priced by the page, many freelance writers are paid by the word, and illustrating is sometimes priced by the square foot.

Federal, state, and local governments use supply contracts, which are priced this way and are used for services as well as for commodities and other goods. They are generally annual contracts, although some are for longer periods with annual options. Regardless of what they are called, they all fit the indefinite-quantity category and are priced on some kind of unit basis.

This arrangement is a convenient one, for it enables you to simply terminate the services of anyone whose service or product is unsatisfactory, and to end or extend the services to suit your needs (the "escape hatch"). This method is commonly used in contracting, and as compared with the competitive-proposal method, it has the advantage of giving you a great deal of freedom and flexibility.

HYBRID METHODS

The government sometimes uses the best features of both the bid and the proposal methods of procurement in what is known generally as a *two-step procurement*, explained earlier. There is a variation on this method that relies on the use of capabilities statements to qualify future bidders or proposers as those who will be the only ones from whom bids or proposals will be accepted. The chief difference is that this latter procedure is generally used to develop a bidders' list for some future and usually not yet well-defined procurement, whereas the two-step method is generally used for a definite, immediate procurement.

GOVERNMENT VERSUS PRIVATE-SECTOR PROCUREMENT

There is one important fact to be observed here: Much of what has been described is taken from the methods pursued by federal, state, and local governments because they represent a rich pool of examples, based largely on codes established by a special committee of the American Bar Association and many of which are emulated by private-sector organizations. However, government procurement is always fixed by statute, a constraint that does not normally exist in procurement by organizations in the private sector. Therefore, you are free, if you are in the private sector, to modify and adjust these methods in any way that suits your own needs and desires, within the policy constraints of your own organization.

There Is Always a Product

It must be noted that, although consulting is basically a service and most of the contract forms cited here are designed to contract for services, there is always a product of some sort. Creation of the product may be the main objective of the project or it may be only incidental, but there *is* a product, even if it is only a report. It would be unacceptable in most organizations to spend money without being able to produce something tangible as an outcome, something to document and justify the expenditure. In many cases that product, whatever it is, is the only thing that represents value received for the expenditure.

For example, you may spend thousands of dollars to have a special computer program written for you. The program itself, in whatever form it is delivered (e.g., tape or disk), is the main objective of the project. It and the documentation, especially the manual, are the products. On the other hand, if you hire a consultant to simply operate your system or help design the hardware configuration, it is the service itself that is the main objective. However, you do want a written report from the consultant documenting his or her recommendations and rationales.

Specifying the Product

Stipulating and describing the product are always important steps in your request, guiding respondents in what you require, and also in the contract, specifying what the contractor is liable for. More than a few unsatisfactory performances and subsequent contract disputes have resulted from the failure to specify the physical product required.

Specificity is a must. It is not enough to state that a final report or manual is required. You must specify what is to be in the report or manual. It is, in fact, a good idea to furnish a format and an outline. Certainly, as an absolute minimum, you must specify what kinds of information you require.

That specification must be quantitative as well as qualitative if you wish to avoid problems. For example, suppose you envision a manual of about 150 pages and sincerely believe that nothing much smaller will suffice, but you fail to specify that estimate as a requirement and the contractor delivers a manual of 60 pages. (You may be fortunate enough to encounter exceptions, but do not expect most contractors to do more than whatever they believe to be the minimum necessary.) You can accept what you think is inadequate or you can demand more. You may get more without a struggle, but you may also have a dispute, because since neither the RFP/work statement nor the contract specified a number of pages, the contractor believes you have no right to demand more than you got.

On the other hand, it is possible that there will be cases in which it is difficult for you to specify, much less quantify, the end product of the work. After all, it is because you need the expertise of the consultant specialist that you have invited proposals and committed yourself to awarding a contract. So it is not unreasonable to expect the proposer to specify what he or she proposes to deliver as an end product in both quantitative and qualitative terms. Unfortunately, if you did not specify the end product in the RFP, most proposers are not likely to specify it in their proposals, so you often wind up in a dispute that could (and should) have been foreseen and avoided. The way to avoid this is simple: Require specifically, in your specifications of what must be included in the proposals, detailed quantitative and qualitative descriptions of proposed end products. Then you can choose those which you deem to be most suitable.

Incidentally, it has become a practice, when proposals are submitted, to include the proposal as the *schedule* (specification of the agreement) of the contract. That is a great time- and labor-saver, and therefore it is an excellent example to follow. Treat proposals as though they were the contract itself, for they often are.

Pricing

If you are in government, you will normally be required to have the proposer submit separate technical and cost proposals. The idea is to evaluate each technical proposal on its technical merits, without being influenced by costs. Only when the technical evaluation is complete are the evaluators permitted to see the cost proposal.

Private-sector organizations have no such stricture, of course, unless it is by internal fiat, but you should try to ignore the costs while evaluating the worthiness of the proposal and the proposer. (You can emulate the government example by requiring that costs be submitted in a separate document in a sealed envelope and withholding examination of that until you have made your judgments of technical worthiness.)

Despite the importance of the specification of what must be included in the proposal, the statement of work (or SOW) you provide (and/or the item description, where the end product is of great importance) is probably the most critical element of the solicitation. No other element of a solicitation for expert help and services has quite as much influence on the results as does the statement of work.

THE TWO IMPORTANT CHARACTERISTICS OF THE STATEMENT OF WORK

The SOW is a key item, the central element in any solicitation sent out for specialized services of any kind, whether those services are for writing an annual report, reorganizing an office system, or designing a faster airplane. It *is* the direct solicitation, explaining what you want. It should therefore come as no surprise that a poorly designed or poorly written SOW is likely to produce poorly designed and poorly written responses. (In federal procurement, an overall average of about two-thirds of all proposals received are rejected as nonresponsive, but no one knows how many of these are nonresponsive because the SOWs are poor ones.)

There are two features that characterize poor statements and two others that characterize good statements. Badly designed requests represent two extremes:

1. They have too much detail, with the statements heavily weighted according to the requestor's ideas, some of which may be biased unreasonably.
2. They have too little information, with the statements quite vague, making it difficult—almost impossible in many cases—for the bidder or proposer to be completely responsive.

These are self-defeating defects, serious even when you are quite sure of what you want and your need is a simple one. They are even more serious when you are relying on the respondents to help diagnose your problems and offer creative ideas for their solution.

The ideal SOW falls at some midpoint between these extremes and exhibits the following two major characteristics:

1. It is entirely definitive of your need or problem and/or your major objective, leaving the respondent no doubts or uncertainties about them.
2. It solicits and encourages ideas, suggestions, and recommendations from those responding to the request, and it is designed to allow ample room for them.

Admittedly, in an imperfect world a SOW rarely meets the ideal or comes even close to it. However, in any SOW you write you should strive to avoid the extremes and fall as close as possible to the midpoint, remembering that it is very much in your own interest to do so.

ELEMENTS OF THE SOW

Of course, SOWs will vary widely from one case to another, according to a sea of variables. (Some relevant information, for example, may be confidential and will be withheld from the statement, although imparted later to the successful bidder, and some is political and would embarrass and possibly compromise the requestor were it revealed.) However, most complete and well-written statements normally include certain basic elements. The following are typical:

1. A clear and complete description or definition of your need. (The term *need* implies the need to solve a *problem* or

satisfy a *requirement.*) This should be in as objective a set of terms as possible.

2. A summary of all available facts upon which the need is based (e.g., symptoms).
3. All data that a contractor will need to respond intelligently (e.g., factual accounts, outlines, reports, drawings, charts, etc.).
4. A listing or description of constraints, special conditions, your biases and preferences, and anything else that will affect the work to be done and, therefore, the response to your request.
5. A clear description of the desired main end product(s) (e.g., a final report or a formal verbal presentation).
6. A clear description of interim products (e.g, written progress reports or drafts of a document).
7. A schedule of key events, especially the final completion or delivery date.

Providing all these items is not quite as simple and uncomplicated as it may appear. Some extended discussion will make this clear.

Defining Your Need

The earlier discussion of objective analysis via the methods of value management is appropriate here since these methods are designed to encourage objective, unemotional judgment. Let us suppose that you have a product that is not selling well, although you know it to be a fine product. (You know that because *you* conceived and created the product yourself, so you know that it is easily the equal of any directly competitive product.) You believe that your need is to create a more convincing explanation of the product's merits to be presented to the public via your print, radio, and television advertising. What this product really needs, you are quite sure, is better copy so the public will *understand* its merits. And because you *know* that to be the case, you make it quite clear in your SOW that you want a high-powered marketing expert, one who understands the importance of *copy,* to come aboard and handle this campaign to put your product on the map where it belongs!

You have several strikes against you already: It is your product—you conceived and created it—so you have a stake in it. Your personal prestige is involved, or so you perceive it, and so it would be remarkable if you could be truly objective about it. Another strike is that you have already decided that the failure of the public to understand the merits of your product is the reason for its lackluster performance in the marketplace. You are oriented to advertising copy as the key to success or failure in the marketplace.

Of course, it is quite possible that your product has done poorly for any of several other reasons: Pricing may be all wrong, media choices may be bad ones, packaging may be poorly conceived, distribution may be inefficient, or any number of other bad choices and decisions may have been made. Even if it *is* a copy problem, it is not necessarily the sales arguments that are failing; perhaps the basic motivation itself is badly conceived.

The real point is that you are denying yourself the objectivity that a consultant can bring to your problem by deciding in advance what your problem is when you really do not know what it is. You are committing the classic mistake of confusing the problem with its symptoms. The symptom is that the product is not selling. You have assumed that the problem is poor advertising copy. That may be true, but it is far from clear that it *is* true. The fact is that you know only what the symptom is. What you really need is a marketing consultant whose first mission is to determine what the problem is—why the product is not selling—

and whose second mission is to devise a solution to whatever the problem proves to be. However, you might be well advised to first assign a consultant to determine what the problem *is* and reserve judgment on the next step until then. Frequently, projects are divided into two phases. The first phase is intended to investigate and diagnose the problem. The consultant then presents results to the client before beginning the second phase, so the client can consider the need in light of the information developed in the first phase.

To design your program in that manner, you must somehow manage to be objective enough to recognize that you are dealing with a symptom or set of symptoms and do not yet know what the core problem is, at least not with any great certainty.

That is really the essence of the matter: managing to be truly objective in identifying your need so that you can construct a logical approach to satisfying it. That in itself is an excellent reason to avoid using the term *problem* and use the term *need* instead. Use of *problem* tends to lure you into the trap of making unwarranted, snap judgments as you try to make your own diagnosis without having enough data to work with. In fact, you should always consider the possibility—even probability—that what you, as an executive or manager, generally regard as the problem, is what the individual charged with finding a solution must regard as the major symptom. That is so often the case that it is probably wise to refrain from offering your own definition of your problem at all.

Supplying the Facts

You can gain a great deal by simply describing your need in terms of what you actually can observe, what you know to be a fact. If you provide a complete and detailed list of everything you know to be a verifiable fact, it will provide several distinct benefits.

Bear in mind that problem identification (troubleshooting) involves specific steps in all cases:

1. Observing all visible and audible symptoms.
2. Organizing symptoms and associating them logically.
3. Learning and noting any significant associated history.
4. Forming a theory based on the foregoing.
5. Verifying the theory.

This is what any competent consultant you retain will do when there is a problem to be solved. What you supply or fail to supply in your SOW can aid or retard the process, save you time and money or cost you time and money. Hence, the importance of providing complete and accurate details in describing symptoms and the wisdom of withholding your own judgment of the problem.

If you do a good job of supplying this information you will be rewarded with far better proposals than would otherwise be the case. In fact, in many cases you will find that the experienced consultant will offer at least a tentative diagnosis of the problem in responding to your proposal request. When you have several proposals to study, you have a much better basis for deciding whether any of the suggested definitions are correct.

Additional Data

In many cases there is additional material that will aid the consultant in responding to your request. For example, if you want a manual, report, or training program written and have done some advance thinking about it and prepared a rough draft or outline (or even a partial draft that reflects your ideas about what you want), you will probably get better proposals and a lower estimate of costs if you supply that material as part of the work statement.

The same consideration applies to other ancillary materials such as drawings, charts, and published papers that are relevant to your need. If you save the consultant time in researching, the result will be a better proposal and probably a better price.

Special Constraints and Conditions

Failure to make absolutely clear the factors that will directly affect the work can lead to contract disputes. For example, suppose there are individuals or facilities to which the consultant will require access but those are not available during normal working hours—that is, the consultant is compelled to work evenings or weekends to gain necessary access to those individuals or facilities. That is likely to affect the costs, and it should have been anticipated and stipulated in advance. Or suppose some company policy mandates frequent in-process reviews and conferences after each phase of work and that was not stipulated. Again, an excellent opportunity for a later dispute.

Descriptions of Interim and End Products

Unfortunately, a great many SOWs describe the end products that are required rather vaguely, and they fall down even more in the matter of quantitative definitions than in qualitative ones. For example, the work statement may describe the kind of information required in a report but fail to give a clue as to how large a report is envisioned, how it should be bound, how many copies should be delivered, and other details.

It is entirely understandable that this should happen, for the client is asking the consultant to propose a project. It is not unreasonable to assume that it is the respondent's responsibility to provide such information, to provide many of the specifications. However, respondents may also neglect to be completely specific about the end products they propose to deliver, or they may be reluctant to make absolute commitments.

The cure for the problem is quite simple: Make it a point to require that the respondent offer precise and complete descriptions—qualitative and quantitative—of proposed end products.

All of this applies also to interim products such as progress reports and draft manuscripts or programs. They are not likely to be specified with any precision or completeness unless precision and completeness are required.

Schedule of Key Events

Very much the same considerations apply to schedules. Quite often, the writers of SOWs do not project their thoughts into the future to anticipate the circumstances that are likely to occur when the project gets under way. As a result, they often project schedules that prove to be impractical, especially when there is to be a series of interrelated and interdependent events. For example, here is a typical proposed schedule that is likely to prove troublesome in the reality:

First (kickoff) meeting:	April 15
Deliver preliminary plan:	May 4
Client review, approval:	May 11
Deliver draft manuscript:	June 21
Client review complete:	July 5
Deliver revised draft:	August 5
Client review, approval:	August 12
Deliver 50 printed copies:	September 20

There are several problems with this schedule. First, it is by no means certain that the contract will be awarded and work will begin on the scheduled date; things of that sort have an uncomfortable way of slipping. Second, there is no way to be certain that the client can complete the reviews by the dates indicated; it would be surprising, in fact, if the client did not need more time. So aside from the fact that the client may very well have to spend time revising the dates, there, again, the scene is set for later disputes.

Here is a way to minimize these possibilities:

First (kickoff) meeting:	5 days after award
Deliver preliminary plan:	21 days after award
Client review, approval:	10 days after submittal
Deliver draft manuscript:	30 days after approval
Client review complete:	10 days after submittal
Deliver revised draft:	30 days after review completed
Client review, approval:	10 days after submittal
Deliver 50 printed copies:	21 days after approval

This frees the schedule from the calendar and frees the consultant from dates committed in advance—should the client require more than 10 days for review, for example.

Even so, there is still a pronounced flaw in this second schedule, and it is this: The word *day* is not defined. Are these calendar days or working days? That makes a large difference, and the definition should be specified by stipulation in the schedule itself.

Chapter Six

Evaluating Proposals

Evaluation of proposals is both arduous and unavoidably subjective to a large degree. Still, it is possible to reduce the total effort—to introduce a degree of efficiency into the process—and to establish guidelines and methodology to incorporate some degree of objectivity.

THE GENERAL APPROACH TO EVALUATION

When major projects and contracts are at stake and major proposals are required, the client calls for a large number of copies of each proposal. That is because a large number of people must be assigned to study and evaluate the proposal. The reasons for this are easy to understand. For one thing, the proposals are far too large and cover too wide a diversity of subjects to be read and studied by a single individual; major proposals can run to hundreds—even thousands—of pages in some cases. No individual is expected to be expert enough in all matters to be able to evaluate the entire proposal in these cases. In fact, there might be a team of experts, rather than an individual, assigned to each major area. Typically, the separate proposal areas or project functions to which assignments for proposal evaluation might be made include at least the following:

- Technical approach
- Plan
- Management
- Staffing
- Qualifications
- Resources
- References
- Special items

That last area, special items, can vary widely. If, for example, the expert service required is in some abstruse or unusually specialized field—celestial mechanics, for example—someone especially well qualified in that field will be required to make a realistic and dependable assessment of the proposed work. In may cases, that will mean seeking out and retaining a consultant, or even several consultants, to help evaluate proposals. (Hiring consultants to help evaluate proposals is not an unusual practice, just as retaining consultants to help write requests for proposals is not at all unusual.)

Within each general area an entire set of criteria would be designated for review—for example, feasibility, quality of experience, relevance of experience, adequacy of resources, quality of proposed staff, suitability of schedules and deliverable items proposed, and other such factors.

The difference between evaluating a major proposal and an average one, or even an informal one, is merely one of degree, not of kind. All or most of the factors listed here should be considered when evaluating proposals. Obviously, for an average proposal, evaluation will not be a heavily staffed project, and when the proposal is a small one, you might do the entire job yourself. However, whether you do the job yourself or assign it to others, some guidelines are necessary if the evaluation is to be orderly and efficient. In fact, evaluating proposals is somewhat analogous to evaluating resumés of job applicants: It is first a screening process—acceptance of the qualified and rejection of the unqualified—and finally a selection process.

THE INITIAL SCREENING

It is not unusual to get several dozen proposals in response to an advertised solicitation, especially when the statement of work is written in a clear and easily understandable manner. Good SOWs are a great inducement to respond to such solicitations, for they make responding appear to be relatively easy to do, misleading as that impression may be. (Conversely, a difficult-to-understand request for proposals discourages responses because it appears to be difficult to respond to.) Many RFPs elicit 50 or more responses, and that results in a massive effort to read and evaluate them unless some kind of screening process is employed. Only a little experience in reading and evaluating proposals quickly demonstrates the need for screening. The reasons for this follow.

Responsiveness

It may be taken as an article of faith that in most cases a large portion of the responses to a solicitation are grossly unsuitable for one reason or another. Government agencies find, for example, that often as many as nine out of ten proposal responses are not truly responsive to the request and cannot be given serious consideration. Even on a broad average, two out of three proposals are found to be nonresponsive.

Nonresponsiveness takes many forms and occurs for many reasons. Here are a few of the reasons many proposals prove to be nonresponsive and a few examples of the types of nonresponsive proposals you are likely to get:

- Some nonresponsive proposers do not even try to write a proposal. Instead, they send along a collection of brochures or, in some cases, a single, rather thick and elaborate brochure, with a form letter.
- There are always respondents who are not truly qualified but hope to muddle through somehow, or perhaps believe that the award will be made on a kind of lottery basis. In any case, these respondents assume that there is little to lose in making a try for the brass ring. Depending on how clever or glib they are as writers, you may put a great deal of effort into studying their proposals before you realize that you are wasting your time.
- Along the same lines as the unqualified respondents are those who write responses assembled swiftly from boilerplate materials that are used over and over, on the assump-

tion that if they a submit a large enough number of these generic proposals the laws of probability will work to produce an occasional victory. If the boilerplate is good enough, these proposals may prove to be great time-wasters also.

- There are some who cannot or will not try to really study and digest your SOW and the rest of your solicitation package. At least it appears that they have not really read the material, for they send in what seems to be a serious proposal but apparently in response to someone else's request. You do not recognize a response to your own need in it, and you waste time reviewing it before you recognize it for what it is.
- There are many proposers whose proposals are nonresponsive in far less obvious and more subtle ways. Evidently, they are unable to provide what you need, and they try to change your rules, even to the extent of trying to rewrite your SOW. Again their cleverness and glibness affect how much of your time is wasted in evaluating their proposals.
- Finally, there are proposers whose responses are, or appear to be, quite close to what you want but are still nonresponsive because they offer a program or set of services that simply does not match your need completely. These can be divided into subordinate classes, including those who have submitted acceptable plans but have deficiencies in other areas: The plan they propose is not truly right for you, they do not appear to be qualified or capable of executing their apparently excellent plan, or they appear to be generally unreliable as contractors.

Three Important Criteria

There are three general areas in which you ought to scrutinize and evaluate prospective contractors:

1. The apparent soundness of the plan they propose
2. Their apparent qualifications and capabilities for executing the plan
3. Their dependability as contractors

Be aware in advance that contracts go to the best proposal writers, who may or may not be the best contractors. Be aware, too, that there are consultants who are expert proposal writers and who are often retained by organizations to perform that function. The organization, with or without the help of a consultant, may be able to turn out an excellent appraisal, technical approach, proposed program, and related presentations in its proposal, but you need assurance that the proposer can also *execute* that plan and is *dependable* as a contractor. Alas, there are proposers who can produce excellent proposals and are capable technically and professionally, but are not reliable. Their practice is to start many projects, leave them unfinished, and keep as many going at one time as they can. In short, their business philosophy appears to focus on *winning* contracts, rather than *performing* on them.

You may have noticed that the descriptions given here of typical nonresponsiveness progress generally from the ludicrously and even obviously nonresponsive proposal to the nearly right one. That is, they progress from responses that can be rejected immediately, even without a complete reading, to those that require careful study before making a decision.

It hardly seems worthwhile, in light of this, to devote equal time to all responses; much of that time and effort would presumably be wasted on proposals that are unlikely to be acceptable. A more logical method is to attack proposal evaluation as a process to be carried out in stages. To achieve some degree of efficiency, at least three and possibly four screening phases should be used along the following lines:

1. First phase: Quickly screen out the obviously unsuitable and unacceptable responses.
2. Second phase: Do a closer screening and eliminate the responses that appear to be acceptable at first reading but on closer study prove to be not quite acceptable.
3. Third phase: Study the remaining responses—and it should normally be relatively few—to make final selections of those that are acceptable or *can be made so.*
4. Fourth phase: Conduct best-and-final interviews and negotiations, and/or make the final choice and award the contract.

THE MATTER OF COSTS

In the federal system of procurement, costs cannot be described or explained in the original technical proposal. Costs are to be submitted in a separate volume, a cost proposal, and evaluators are not to know the costs until they have completed their technical evaluations. The purpose of this is to enable evaluators to be objective in their technical evaluations and to remain uninfluenced in their judgments by knowledge of costs. In that system, cost is then a final consideration.

In the private sector, that may or may not be the practice. Usually, it will not be, at least not for the smaller projects, so that anyone evaluating proposals may know and be influenced by the costs quoted. Therefore, cost might or might not be among the early screening criteria—you might or might not discard proposals purely on that basis. Yet, there are other aspects of cost to be considered and, again, it is helpful to look at the federal system to gain insights into this question.

Government procurement regulations are quite voluminous, and so they allow a great deal of interpretation and resultant policy making by contracting officials. There are several approaches to evaluating costs and pursuing the cost issue in this arena:

- Award the contract or open negotiations with the lowest bidder among those whose proposals are acceptable.
- Request best-and-final offers (bids) of those whose proposals are acceptable, and negotiate with the low bidder.
- Request best-and-final offers from only the lowest bidder, the three lowest bidders, the proposer with the best technical score, or the three proposers with the best technical scores, or use other approaches following this general pattern.
- Offer all proposers an opportunity to improve their proposals and cost estimates.
- Assign an actual weight to costs (e.g., maximum number of points for lowest costs to zero points for highest costs) to be added to points awarded for the technical proposal.
- Use a formula to calculate a cost per technical point, and award the contract to the proposer with the lowest cost per technical point.
- Make a simple subjective judgment on cost as a factor, as long as cost does not exceed budget. (Usually, award the contract to the proposer with the highest technical score, if the costs are within budget.)

These guidelines include cost as a factor, but you will, of course, adapt them to whatever methods you decide to use.

THE FIRST SCREEN

It seems logical to assume that at least the first phase, the rough screening of the more or less obviously unsuitable responses, can be carried out informally on the basis of simple judgment. Still, unless you want to do this yourself—and that should not be necessary, nor would it be an efficient use of your time—you need some criteria upon which to base this immediate rejection.

The general criterion is responsiveness. But to enable a subordinate to make the judgment of responsiveness for you in even a first-phase, coarse screening, you must supply some kind of guidance and methodology. Following is a suggested set of guidelines to serve as the first screen. That is, the response must conform to these broad standards to survive the first scrutiny. (Of course, you would have armed the screener with a definition of items to be identified.)

1. There must be a letter of transmittal identifying the enclosure as a formal response to a specific request.
2. The response must identify and address the need or requirement specified in the solicitation and statement of work. (Printed brochures are acceptable as enclosures, attachments, exhibits, or portions of the proposal, but are not acceptable as the basic response itself.)
3. The response must be generally in the format specified in and required by the solicitation. (For example, if the solicitation requires double-spaced copy, single-spaced copy is not acceptable; if there is a page limitation, responses in excess of that are not acceptable.)
4. The estimated cost must be within the competitive range, and it must appear to be close enough to your budget to furnish reasonable hope for satisfactory negotiation.

Rejection of responses as dictated by these considerations is based on the assumption that a respondent who is unable or unwilling to comply with basic requirements offers a proposal that is not worth reading.

These are mere suggestions; you may wish to be more generous or less so. In government procurement, each contracting official views this first phase differently. At one extreme are those who go along with summary rejection of responses that are obviously out of tune with the specific requirements, while at the other extreme are those who believe that everyone who has taken the trouble to respond ought to be given a chance to amend the response after being advised of shortcomings. There are contracting officials who impose their chosen policies on their agencies, and there are others who have a laissez-faire attitude and permit the people who request the proposals and make the technical evaluations to run their evaluations as they see fit. There are, of course, good arguments for each of these approaches; you will have to decide which is in your own best interest.

Worksheet and Checklist

To help you conduct this first screening, refer to the worksheet shown in Figure 6–1. It lists the major items to be checked. Of course, you can modify and adapt this to your own ideas and needs. The weighting is my own estimate. You may wish to change it.

Space is provided for comments. No standardized plan can anticipate all possibilities—especially not one that is as generalized as this one.

THE SECOND SCREEN

The second screen is, by definition, applied to all proposals that have survived the first screen. These are, presumably, proposals that have survived a full reading; they probably comprise less than one-half of the original total. These must be given a formal

The Second Screen

ITEM TO BE CHECKED	CRITERION	PASS	NO PASS	WEIGHT
Letter of transmittal	Your identifying number or description	☐	☐	10
Introduction identifying and addressing need	Need as defined in RFP and SOW	☐	☐	50
Conformity with format required	Required format defined	☐	☐	20
Cost within competitive range	Competitive range defined	☐	☐	20

COMMENTS

Figure 6–1. Worksheet for First Screen.

evaluation, of course, to verify their responsiveness in all respects. I suggest that the checklist shown in Figure 6–2 be applied (directly or with whatever modifications would adapt it to your own purposes) in screening responses through a second round.

1. The response must exhibit a clear understanding of your requirement as you stated it, but not by simply echoing your own description. Rather, it must restate your require-

ITEM TO BE CHECKED	CRITERION	PASS	NO PASS	WEIGHT
Understanding of requirement	Statement of the requirement	☐	☐	15
Extended discussion	Judgment call	☐	☐	10
Approach and technical arguments	Judgment call	☐	☐	15
Suitability of program proposed	Judgment call	☐	☐	20
Schedule and deliverables	Compare with those anticipated	☐	☐	10
Assessed capability of contractor to deliver	Judgment and reference check	☐	☐	10
Dependability of contractor	Judgment and reference check	☐	☐	10
Reasonableness of costs	Compare with budget	☐	☐	10

COMMENTS

____

____

____

____

____

Figure 6–2. Worksheet for Second Screen.

ment in some way that provides assurance of true understanding.

2. The understanding must be further demonstrated by an extended discussion, with persuasive technical arguments and an approach that appears to be workable and likely to produce the desired results.
3. The proposed approach and arguments must be translated into a specific action program that is a logical consequence of the approach and arguments.
4. The proposed schedule and description of the deliverable items must be entirely compatible with your own stated requirement and conditions.
5. The costs must be within the competitive range.
6. The proposer must have shown a good grasp of the management requirements and responsibilities of the project and must have presented what appears to be a suitable management plan.
7. The proposer should have presented what appears to be a reasonable case of qualifications: appropriate and adequate resources, suitable experience, and acceptable staff assignments and individual resumés.
8. Finally, the proposer must have offered evidence of reliability in following through and carrying a project to completion.

THE THIRD SCREEN

A third screening is certainly not a must; you may or may not find it necessary. It depends largely on how large and important the project is and the size and number of proposals submitted. It also depends on how many proposals have survived the earlier screening and remain for active consideration in the final stages. It is possible that in some cases there are so few proposals remaining that you can now proceed to final decision making, or perhaps you have found one or two so outstandingly excellent that you decide to consider only those. However, for purposes of discussion, assume that enough nominally acceptable proposals remain to make it necessary to winnow the list further before trying to make the final assessments and select a proposer for award.

Obviously, this is going to be the most difficult screening. You are dealing with proposals approximately equal to each other, all apparently acceptable and none decisively outstanding. You are down to the finest discriminations.

Cost is always a major consideration. If your system is such that evaluators are aware of the cost estimates in each proposal, you may have already eliminated all proposals with estimated costs beyond the level acceptable to you. Or, as in the case of many government contracting officials, you may have set a maximum level that is greater than your maximum acceptable figure, but not so far in excess of it as to preclude the possibility of negotiating the costs to an acceptable level. For example, suppose that your budget will not permit you to commit more than $150,000 to a project, but you have several excellent proposals that are well above that figure: one at $170,000, another at $210,000, and still another at $345,000. (Yes, the range can easily be that wide and even wider in many cases.)

Probably the average contracting official would agree that there is a reasonable basis for negotiation of a bid that is within 20 percent of your in-house estimate. That is, there is hope of negotiating the $170,000 bid down to $150,000 or less. It is most unlikely that the $345,000 figure—slightly more than 56.5 percent above your budget—could be negotiated down to an acceptable $150,000. The $210,000 bid—a little more than 28.5 percent over budget—is in a gray area. It would take a great deal of negotiating to get that number down to $150,000, presumably, but it does not appear to be a totally forlorn hope. Too, there is always the possibility that the high bidders misunderstood the full nature of the requirement and seriously—but in all honesty—overestimated the effort required. Therefore, according to this kind of reasoning, it is probably worthwhile to have a meeting with each of the proposers to discuss their proposals and explore whether they may wish to make serious revisions to the proposals and cost estimates.

That approach is a matter of policy or individual decision, but it is a successful approach in many cases. Therefore, you may choose not to discard the high bidders' proposals at once, but perhaps place them in a "maybe" file as insurance against the possibility of having no other proposals that are technically acceptable.

The thought might occur to you at this point that if you were aware of each proposer's cost quotations during technical evaluation you would have made the critical decision to reject them or set them aside earlier in the screening process. However, even that is not necessarily true, for this reason: You might have withheld that final judgment until you could see how many proposals you would have left after the first and second screenings. Then, if you still had a number of acceptable proposals within your price range from which to make a final choice, you might decide that it was more efficient to simply discard those of the high bidders and not devote any more time to them. But if you had few other good proposals left—and sometimes that number might be zero—you would then want to consider whether you could work out an acceptable compromise with the author of one of those higher-cost proposals.

So it is probably not wise to make an absolute decision or adopt some absolutely fixed policy standardizing your practices and procedures in this regard. The many possible combinations of circumstances are such that you are well advised to keep your policies rather general and allow a great deal of latitude for judging individual cases on their own merits.

Aside from that, and even if you have had discussions with proposers and obtained their best-and-final offers, you might still have other problems in making the final choices. If you want to standardize your approach and make hard-and-fast rules to simplify your life, these are the avenues most readily open:

1. Award to the low bidder, that is, the lowest final bidder among those with acceptable proposals.
2. Use a strictly objective point system and award to the highest-scoring bidder.
3. Award to the proposer with the highest score for technical quality who can meet your budget requirement.

In the next chapter, the final stages of negotiating and contracting are explored in greater detail.

Chapter Seven

Negotiations and Contracts

Disputes are what contracts are designed to avoid or, at least, to minimize, and the more detailed the contract is, the greater the probability of avoiding disputes. Detailed agreement results from detailed negotiations.

WHAT IS A CONTRACT?

Commonly, when reference is made to *the contract,* it is to a document, a package of paper on which words are written. But a contract is not really a physical object, and it is certainly not a package of paper on which the parties have described and recorded an agreement. The paper merely represents the agreement that is *really* the contract. The chief reason for describing that agreement on paper and signing names to it is to guard against the frailties of human memories and avoid later disputes, if possible, or at least minimize such disputes and render them easier to resolve than might otherwise be the case. It is probably not possible to avoid occasional disputes for at least two reasons. First, it is impossible to anticipate every eventuality. Second, words are not precise instruments of communications; they are mere symbols that each person interprets, and even the most fair-minded and honest of people cannot help but be influenced to at least some small extent by self-interests in their interpretations. Therefore, disputes do arise occasionally, either because some condition or event that could not have been foreseen requires a special interpretation under the terms set forth in the written contract, or because of semantic difficulties when the two parties to the agreement differ as to the meaning of some clause or paragraph.

THE PHYSICAL FORMS OF CONTRACTS

The factors just described are good arguments against verbal agreements. That is not to say that a verbal contract is not a binding one; legally, it is as binding as any written contract. But how does one resolve disputes under verbal contracts? How does one prove that the contract even existed, should proof become necessary? (The late Hollywood mogul, Sam Goldwyn, is alleged to have said, "A verbal contract is not worth the paper it is written on," which is probably a reasonable summation!)

Of course, you do not enter into a contract anticipating disputes. The act of committing a contract to paper, with signatures to bind the parties, is a form of insurance. You hope to never have to say "Read your contract" to the other party. In fact, you would be unwise to contract with anyone without the firm conviction that the other party is acting in good faith and fully intends to honor the agreement in every detail. Contracts that have to be enforced against the will of either party are bad contracts, contracts that never should have been signed.

However, there is the matter of practicality. When large sums of money—perhaps millions of dollars—are at stake, it would be foolish to enter into a contract without thorough study and ample documentation by legal experts of as many details and contingencies as they can anticipate. (This is in addition to and as a result of extended, formal negotiations, of themselves a major expense). But how much trouble and expense are merited for formal documentation of a small program of a few hundred dollars? Certainly not a great deal of time and money can go into formalizing an agreement for a small project. Still, although many small projects are agreed to and executed under verbal or even tacit agreements, it is never a good idea. There are inexpensive methods for documenting agreements. Here are several ways to record an agreement easily, inexpensively, and legally—in fully binding fashion—when the work to be performed does not justify formal negotiations and contracting:

- Purchase orders
- Letters of agreement or understanding
- Other simple forms of agreement

In other words, there are many ways in which a contract can be documented and recorded so as to make it not only binding but contestable and defensible later, which is what the word *binding* really means. The whole purpose of committing a contract to some written form is to establish a clear record and definition of the agreement. The exact form and format of the document created to do this is not the essence of the agreement, and it is of relatively little consequence as long as it is established clearly that the parties have consciously entered into the agreement and the agreement is well defined. The alternatives to the full-blown formal sheaf of bound paper, with its blue covers, staples, and myriad *whereases* and *wherefores*, will be examined next.

Purchase Orders

Purchase orders are probably the most common forms used for small purchases. Most medium-size and large organizations have their own purchase-order forms, preprinted with their names and designed to suit their own needs. Usually, the form has at least three parts, for the following disposition: The original and one copy to the consultant, and the client retains the third copy in a suspense file. The consultant signs and returns the original, or first, copy as an acknowledgment and agreement with what is specified in the order, keeping the second copy for his or her records. In some cases, there is a fourth copy, which the consultant keeps until the work is completed, whereupon the consultant signs it as a claim of completion and invoice and returns it to the client for payment. Other variations are possible; some organizations' purchase orders do not require a signed copy as acknowledgment, since they have received written or verbal acknowledgment by letter or telephone. But the basic method is the same, no matter how much variation there is in details.

Smaller organizations and individual entrepreneurs can buy off-the-shelf purchase order forms from any good stationer, with or without their own names imprinted. These serve equally well, and there are enough different models offered to enable you to select one that suits your needs.

The purchase order must describe what the supplier (consultant, in this case) is to deliver, so some kind of summary statement of work must be presented in the body of the purchase order. That can be abstracted from the consultant's correspondence, capabilities brochure, proposal, or other presentation. Quite frequently it comes from an informal or letter proposal that the consultant submitted earlier, sometimes even from an earlier quotation.

There is another alternative to the formal, printed purchase-order form, one that I use. Inasmuch as I do not do a great deal of buying, I abandoned the use of imprinted, off-the-shelf forms and use a much simpler method instead, an ordinary letterhead with the words *Purchase Order* typed thereon.

This serves as well as any preprinted form, and you can make as many carbons as you wish. If you are using a computer and word processor, you can print out more than one copy and keep your own file copy on disk reducing the paper burden considerably and making it easy to look things up. (Of course, you can always print out another paper copy, if you need one.)

Figure 7–1 is a simple example of such an informal purchase order. The "For" portion is used to describe what I want supplied or done; it is the statement of work or the item description.

Letters of Agreement and Other Forms

Referring to Figure 7–2, you will recall that ponderous, legal documents are not necessary to achieve a binding agreement. Simple letter agreements are satisfactory for smaller contracts, and they are commonly used for the purpose. In fact, in many ways simple letters of agreement are superior to typical purchase orders as contractual forms, for they document the responsibilities and obligations in much more detail. You need only

Herman Holtz
P.O. Box 1731 Wheaton, MD 20902 (301) 649-2499

PURCHASE ORDER

Date:

To:

For:

Figure 7–1. Simple Purchase-Order Form.

address a letter to the consultant, offering the work and the price or agreeing to whatever terms have been suggested earlier. In fact, this is an even simpler form of a letter of agreement that works quite simply.

Here is a typical sequence of events from my own experience that explains the entire process:

Someone from an organization calls or writes me, inquiring into my availability for a lecture, seminar, or consulting assignment and requesting relevant general information.

I respond, answering each question—dates of availability, costs, and other information requested.

I am asked to furnish written information of a more specific

EXCELSIOR
MANUFACTURING, INC.

Johnson City, MD 20900 301 777-0000

AGREEMENT

Consultant: ____
(Name & Address)

Services to be provided (and/or other documents to be included by reference):

____

____

____

Reports/Presentations: ____________________________

On client's Premises ☐ *On consultant's premises* ☐

Other or special arrangements: ____________________

Beginning date: ______ Target completion date: ______

Fee(s): $ _____ per _____ for (no.) _______s. Total: $ ______

Advance retainer: $ ___________ Balance: $ __________

Notes, remarks, special provisions, if any: ____________

____

____

____

____

____

for Excelsior Mfg., Inc. (typed)	Consultant (typed)
________________ (signed)	________________ (signed)
(date)	(date)

Figure 7–2. Simple Letter of Agreement Form.

nature—brochures, biographical data, or even a letter proposal—and I do so.

We exchange further correspondence or telephone conversations, usually on the finer details, since we are now essentially in agreement and expect to do business together.

The client sends me a letter, in duplicate, citing the basic terms and including earlier correspondence or a proposal by reference, asking me to sign and return one copy.

We now have consummated a contractual obligation, as binding as any more formal one.

NEGOTIATIONS AND TERMS

A contract consists of a set of *terms*. That word has many definitions. When a customer asks a supplier to state his or her terms, the customer is usually referring to terms of payment—how much, how soon due, how much discount for cash, how many days "cash" means, and related questions. In a contract, the word is more expansive in its scope and refers to the stated conditions, requirements, obligations, limitations, and other constraints. Terms are, in fact, what negotiations are about, and the contract is a direct consequence of the negotiations. What the contract states (or should state) as its terms is what was agreed upon as a result of the discussions, correspondence, proposals, and negotiations. When there is a contract dispute it is really a dispute over what was agreed to in negotiations and related documents; the words are supposed to explain the agreement. Therefore, negotiations and contracts are essentially inseparable.

As in the case of contract forms and formats, the formality and scope of the negotiations vary widely, from an informal telephone conversation and resultant purchase order to protracted meetings of many people over many days. For example, the contract negotiations for the Fort Custer, Michigan, Job Corps Center, a contract with a face value of approximately $9 million in 1964 dollars, involved 20 people, 10 from the government and 10 from the contractor, the Educational Science Division of U. S. Industries, Inc. Consummation required several all-day meetings of the full staffs and breakout meetings of specialists from each staff to addressing specialized problems and resolve questions. (The proposal for that program ran to nearly 1,000 pages in four separate volumes.)

The informal telephone call and the protracted negotiations are extremes. Most contracts are negotiated on a scale falling somewhere between these extremes, whether they are formal or informal. In fact, it is possible to conduct informal negotiations and not even recognize, at least not consciously, that what you are doing is negotiating! In any case, negotiation is usually a flow process, made up of stages that can be distinguished from one another, but steps that are not always clearly discriminable, tending often to merge. For example, in informal contracting, the first inquiry may actually include negotiation, as the inquirer asks pointed questions such as "What is your best price?" "Is there a discount for cash?" and "What kind of delivery can you offer?" and the respondent asks counter questions such as "How soon do you need this?" and "What quantities are we talking about?" It is thus impossible to state positively where the initial inquiry ends and negotiation begins.

Best-and-Final Offers

In larger and more formal contracting processes, there is often a specific and well-defined negotiation stage. This frequently begins as a "best-and-final" stage, whether that term is used or not. Actually, best-and-final inquiries are not confined to formal negotiation and contracting processes, but are usually a part of every negotiation, no matter how informal. The best-and-final stage is usually entered when the client has tentatively decided to award the contract to an individual or has decided that one or more aspirants are acceptable and now wants to explore the possibilities of improving the price and/or the services to be committed.

That is an important point to bear in mind: Price may be the most important and most frequent main topic and objective of negotiations, but it is not always so: Negotiations frequently concern what products and services are to be provided, what schedules are to be agreed to and specified, what the working relationships are to be, and other conditions in addition to (or instead of) price. These other factors can easily be more important than price, although they usually translate into dollars ultimately.

In a more formal situation, the request of a client for best-and-final offers is often the opening gun of negotiations, although it is not always represented as such. In pursuing contracts with government agencies, for example, proposers submitting best-and-final offers usually do not know the answers to any of the following questions, much as they would like to know them as a help in planning final sales and negotiating strategies:

1. Are others also invited to submit best-and-final offers? If so, how many have been?
2. Will there be further negotiations after best-and-final offers are submitted or will the next step be an award?
3. Will a price reduction truly improve the proposer's probability of winning the contract?

It is unlikely that any client will provide answers to these questions, nor should they, since the uncertainty of the answers is a plus factor in their bargaining position. Proposers must make their own estimates as to the answers. A proposer who is eager to win a contract must make the following worst-case assumptions:

1. Other proposers—many others—have been invited to make best-and-final offers; the contest is still highly competitive.
2. There will be no further negotiations; a contract will be awarded without further contact after best-and-final offers are received and evaluated.
3. Price is a critical factor, and any price reduction will enhance the proposer's position.

Therefore, it is very much in your interest, as the client negotiating to get the best possible terms for yourself, to reveal absolutely nothing that might provide answers to proposers' questions regarding any of the matters suggested here. Not only does inscrutability encourage proposers to offer their best prices and most favorable terms in general, but it leaves you with all your options available for follow-up action. You do not even have to decide in advance whether you will conduct follow-up negotiations; you can wait for the results of this step and then decide whether to make immediate award or conduct additional negotiations.

There are several ways to conduct this phase of the process. I have known clients to contact proposers directly by telephone, letter, or telegram requesting a best-and-final offer by the same medium. However, in my experience, it has been more common to invite the proposer to a meeting to discuss the proposal. (At least that is the ostensible reason for the meeting.) Sometimes a series of questions is provided in advance (or at least an idea of the nature of the questions) to help the proposer decide whom to bring along to the meeting to help answer the questions.

It is also not an uncommon practice to invite the proposer to make a formal or informal presentation to open the meeting, if he or she wishes to. Sometimes proposers choose to make such presentations before sitting down to a discussion. This can give you, the client, some insights into the proposer's views and positions, and thus afford you some bargaining advantage. Quite often, however, proposers anticipate exactly this and choose not to make a presentation in the hope of keeping their position unknown and thereby reaping some negotiating advantage.

There are two basic reasons to ask for best-and-final offers. One is simply that you have several proposals and proposers that are about equally acceptable and attractive as contractors, and you find it expedient to use best-and-final offers as a key to making a final decision. The other is that you have decided on the proposer you want, but you believe you must make an effort to get the price down, either because you find it too high—perhaps over your budget or in-house estimate of the cost—or because you want to feel assured in your own mind that you have been prudent and done an efficient job. (It is also possible that you have several good proposals, all of them priced over your budget, and you must get at least one of them down a bit to get approval for the project in your organization.)

Many clients do not make it known that they are really seeking best-and-final offers (the best prices) when they conduct these meetings; often the invitation to meet is presented as necessary to discuss the proposal. However, it often becomes clear that best-and-final offers are at least one objective of the meeting when the proposer is first asked to document verbal answers with a formal written amendment to the original proposal (the reason for this wise move will become apparent shortly), and then, as if it were a spontaneous afterthought, the client states that an amendment to the cost proposal or cost figures is also acceptable!

In one case I witnessed a client openly—and reluctantly—revealing that the real objective of the meeting was to get the price down. That happened when the client, after a long and tiring meeting, became exasperated at the obtuseness of the consultant, who obviously failed to understand what the meeting was about. Depleted of patience, the client finally shouted, "I am trying to tell you that we would like to do business with you but your price is too high!" That is a faux pas in negotiating tactics, although understandable under the circumstances cited here.

Why the reluctance of clients to reveal the main objective of such meetings? For one thing, it is a better negotiating tactic to reveal as little as possible of what you are thinking to the other party. To do so is to open the door to follow-up questions, the answers to which help the other party, not you, achieve some advantage in the bargaining process. As in playing poker, the more inscrutable you are, the more the other party assumes a worst-case scenario as a basis for his or her reasoning. That is to your advantage.

Not everyone conducts best-and-final negotiations as a separate effort or as a precursor to final negotiations. Many clients begin final negotiations immediately following evaluation of the proposals, often beginning with the most highly rated proposal, regardless of price, and trying to reach agreement on price and other matters. In fact, the questions asked may not touch on costs at all, but focus on other matters, depending on what the client's greatest concerns or needs are.

BASES FOR NEGOTIATION

You must have a position of strength from which to negotiate if you are to be effective. That means that you must have a base of information that is adequate both in quantity and in quality.

For example, unless you have had a great deal of experience in the work for which you are hiring consultants, it is difficult to judge the reasonableness and appropriateness of their costs. However, there is one approach open to you in reviewing costs before and during negotiations: a simple comparison of the effort with the dollars. Whether the technical proposal includes cost figures or not, it is always a good practice to require the proposer to offer a schedule of tasks and hours. This is done by making up a list of the tasks to be performed in your behalf, first, and then estimating the hours required for each task. For example, the schedule for a simple, one-person project might be along the lines shown in Figure 7–3. (Most projects would be somewhat more complicated and sophisticated than this.)

A larger project, one requiring several people and much more effort than the one shown in Figure 7–3, would require a much more elaborate chart, of course. If a staff of several people were required, the chart would reveal who would participate in each task or subtask and for how many hours. Totals would then be presented for each task and subtask, for each individual participating, and for the project over all, providing a great deal of relevant data.

Such a chart, whether large or small, is an excellent basis for discussing effort and costs. Moreover, it is an excellent indicator of the consultant's technical ability and professionalism, since it indicates the ability (or lack of ability) to plan in detail and the honesty of purpose to reveal the grand technical strategy. This kind of information is also an excellent aid to judging the appropriateness of the costs. No matter what form the costs are presented

TASK/SUBTASK	NUMBER OF HOURS REQUIRED
Kickoff Project	
Initial meeting w/client	4
Main Analysis	
Gather all data	24
Organize and analyze data	40
Write preliminary report	32
Make Presentation and Recommendations	8
TOTAL HOURS:	108

Figure 7–3. Schedule of Tasks and Hours.

in, with this kind of information available you can judge hourly rates as well as costs over all. If they appear too high, you can discuss them with the consultant and ask him or her to defend them on the basis of the estimated effort.

The Fine Art of Negotiating

Despite the fact that you are entirely justified in and should use wise strategies to gain every negotiating advantage you can, the objective of negotiating is not to take unfair advantage of or victimize the other party, but to reach a useful agreement. To do otherwise is self-defeating, for no bargain that does not satisfy both parties is worth having made; such contracts invariably result in disputes and other problems. For example, if you manage to impose such harsh terms that the other party suffers unduly, he or she will eventually cut a few corners out of necessity, which will be at least as much to your disadvantage as to the contractor's. And if, even worse, you have managed to win such an advantageous position that the other party is eventually unable to fulfill his or her part of the bargain (cannot complete the contract) both of you have lost.

It is ancient wisdom, but as true as it ever was, that the only good contract is one in which both parties benefit. One gentleman with whom I negotiated more than one contract was as astute and as good a negotiator as any I have ever known: Absolutely nothing in a proposal escaped his attention or was agreed to without discussion and bargaining. Yet, before concluding the talks, this gentleman invariably asked for assurance that I and the others on my team were satisfied and had not been wounded by any agreement we had reached. If we demurred that some condition we had accepted was going to be extremely difficult to live with, he returned to that matter to reopen the discussion and try to solve the problem. Needless to say, while we never got rich on any contract we concluded with him, we were never hurt by or had serious disputes about any such contract either.

It is always a wise policy to negotiate sincerely. Negotiate hard, but be honest, be fair, and work at reaching an agreement both parties can live with. A consultant in dire need of work might permit you to impose unreasonable conditions and hope to somehow muddle through, but it is hazardous to future success to have a contractor who is resentful, believing that he or she was outwitted and victimized. You might not know that your conditions are so unreasonable as to threaten the consultant's ability to perform properly or to evoke concealed but very real feelings of outrage, but you should be alert to real distress on the part of the other party by actually probing for it, if it is not evident of itself. You can follow the example of that fine negotiator I just referred to and seek assurance that the other party agrees that he or she can live with the agreement. Then you can feel confident that you have a good contract, one that both of you have entered into with sincere intent and good will between you.

WRITING THE CONTRACT

Despite the advent of the computer, we are more of a "paper society" than ever. Paper threatens to engulf us, and in many places we make serious efforts to stem the flood by reducing the amount of it required to conduct our activities. One of the areas in which this can be accomplished with some degree of effectiveness is contracting.

The contract for a major undertaking, heavy with its terms and conditions and the ponderous language of legal experts, can be a formidable document running to hundreds of pages. One convenient way of limiting size of a contract is to invoke other documents, including them in the contract by reference.

For example, when you have accepted a consultant's detailed

proposal, you have a document that stipulates everything or nearly everything you want included in the contract schedule. It would be wasteful in the extreme to copy all that language into another format called a *schedule* simply to create another ponderous bundle of bound paper. Including the proposal by reference enables you to create a contract with a rather simple contractual form that invokes the technical and cost proposals as part of the contract.

Of course, it is not the entire technical proposal that is included in the contract, but only that portion presenting the specific details of the program proposed.

It is in the interest of being able to do this that I recommend requiring proposers to document changes and additions to their proposals by providing either separate amendments or revised proposals. In fact, when a proposer does that he or she is speeding up the contracting process by simplifying the paperwork, to your mutual benefit. This method is so effective that many large government contracts consist, essentially, of a single page (a form) and the relevant proposals (cost and technical), with amendments and modifications.

CONTRACT TYPES AND FORMS

Just as there are two basic methods of procurement, negotiated (competitive proposals) and cost-competitive (sealed bids), there are two basic types of contracts, fixed-price and variable- or indefinite-price. And just as there are several hybrids and variations of procurement methods, there are hybrids and variations of contract types.

The contract type chosen has nothing to do with the procurement method. A negotiated procurement can lead to either a fixed- or variable-price contract, just as a sealed bid can. The fixed-price contract is rather uncomplicated; it is what its name implies, a well-defined and specific obligation by the client to pay a specific amount of money for a specific effort and/or product provided by the other party. The other kind of contract varies considerably. Here are a few examples of the names by which they are known, which may or may not furnish clues to the services/goods/types of contracts to which they refer:

- Indefinite-quantity (supply) contract
- Time-and-material contract
- Task-order ("call") contract
- Labor-hour contract
- Basic ordering agreement
- Cost-reimbursement contract

Cost reimbursement is not often found in the private sector but is associated primarily with government contracts, especially those for military research and development (R & D). It is used in situations in which the client cannot provide enough information to enable the bidder to make a reasonable estimate of cost. However, to discourage unnecessary expansion of the contract base, the client fixes the fee or profit the contractor can earn, regardless of cost. Unfortunately, it has not had the effect of discouraging contract overruns, so some agencies (NASA, for one) have used contracts that offered award fees—bonuses for bringing in the project ahead of schedule or below estimate, and/or for other especially meritorious achievements. Best known are the so-called cost-plus contracts used to develop new military aircraft, missiles, and other large projects.

Basic ordering agreements, call contracts, task-order contracts, labor-hour contracts, and time-and-material contracts are essentially all the same, similar philosophically to indefinite-quantity or supply contracts except that they are primarily for services rather than for products. They usually involve what people in the trade refer to as a laundry list of services and/or products to be delivered at preestablished rates, such as hourly rates, for each kind of service or type of consultant required, and they may also list overtime rates. The client issues a task order each time something is required, and the contractor prepares an estimate using the rates established. When the client approves the estimate (or negotiates an agreement if the estimate is found unacceptable without discussion), the client issues a purchase order or a work order and work begins. The rates established by the contract are generally the billing rates, so they include overhead and profit.

As an example, the organization I managed won such a contract with the computer services division of the U.S. Postal Service. The laundry list enumerated a variety of computer models and computer languages with which familiarity was required and asked for hourly rates for a variety of computer specialists such as junior and senior programmers, systems analysts, engineers, and designers. The Postal Service then called on the group regularly, via task orders, to help solve a variety of problems and perform many kinds of services.

Chapter Eight

Cost Guidelines: What Should the Services Cost You?

It is inevitably difficult to verify the reasonableness or appropriateness of any quoted prices, but there are a few guidelines, some of which are suggested here.

STANDARD RATES AND FEES

Plastic surgeons, I had reason to learn not long ago, appear to have a "flat-rate manual" along the lines of automobile repair shops. All of the plastic surgeons whose rates I researched quoted very much the same prices for at least the most popular procedures: a "nose-job," an eyelift, a breast enhancement, a breast reduction, and other human-body modifications and repairs that fall into distinct and separate categories. However, if there is any equivalent situation for consultants and consulting, I have not yet discovered it. Still, it is possible to make a few generalizations as guidelines to aid you in judging the suitability of consultant's quotations.

A decade ago, before the most recent inflationary surges, it would have been realistic to estimate the average journeyman rate of an independent consultant at approximately $500 a day. Consultants' rates cited then by California consultant-trainer Howard Shenson (based on his reported survey), formed a fairly tight grouping around that figure, although they tended to be slightly below it more often than above it. That is not to say that there were not many consultants charging less than that or at least a few who commanded higher rates; there were then and there are now a few specialists who are able to command extraordinarily high rates for one reason or another. However, I would estimate that the average day rate today has ascended by at least 50 percent, so that you are likely to find relatively few experienced and able independent consultants willing to bill much below $750 to $1,000 a day or even a bit higher. Again, that is not to say that you might not find able consultants charging less and others charging more. Rates may vary as a consequence of at least the following factors:

1. The area and its general cost of living. A consultant in New

York or Washington is likely to cost somewhat more than one in Dubuque or Little Rock.

2. The technical or professional field. A nuclear physicist consulting in his or her field will usually have a higher day rate than a public relations specialist.
3. The individual's personal qualifications. Academic degrees, professional achievements, personal fame or image in profession, and other such factors have their effect on the rates charged.
4. The individual's personal situation. Some consultants have fluid rates and will quote more favorable rates when they are especially in need of work assignments than when they have enough work to keep them busy.
5. The competitive situation. Consultants who are knowingly bidding against ample competition often tend to sharpen their pencils with special enthusiasm when quoting.
6. The general economic situation. All consultants may be especially energetic in sharpening their pencils when the economy is in a recessionary period. Still, even that bit of knowledge offers you some aid in judging the appropriateness of day rates quoted. For example, should you be quoted rates that are significantly below the $500 to $750 bracket it should inspire you to verify that individual's credentials. On the other hand, should you be quoted a considerably higher rate than that, you also ought to verify the individual's credentials and try to determine why he or she presumes to merit that high rate.

Of course, when there are many proposals and/or quotations, you have another tool for judging them in that you can make comparative evaluations. You should find most of the quotations falling within some coherent range. That represents a form of group estimating. If eight out of ten proposers have quoted day rates within 10 percent of, say, $750, the ones who have quoted significantly higher or lower rates obviously merit skeptical, or at least critical, scrutiny.

OVERHEAD AND OTHER BURDENS

Bear in mind, that the cited day rates are also *billing* rates, the rates you are charged for the service. That is, they include the consultant's overhead and other burdens—advertising, taxes, office rent, telephone, travel, insurance, and other costs of doing business. In other words, those other costs are concealed within the day rate, but they are nevertheless real costs. The consultant may have invested several thousand dollars as marketing overhead in his or her efforts to win the contract, and those dollars are reflected in the day rate. That is, you are not paying $500, $750, $1,000 or more each day directly into the consultant's personal pocket, although it may appear so to you. You are paying the fees to the consultant's enterprise, an entity of its own, which then pays the consultant a salary as an employee and a dividend of profit as a proprietor.

Remember that no one operates any kind of enterprise without a cost burden. When the costs are concealed in a flat billing rate, you may tend to forget that most businesses wind up netting as profit—after salaries and taxes, that is—only 2, 3, or 4 percent. And many one-person enterprises net no true profit, but merely afford the practitioner a modest living. Perhaps it helps to understand that, so that you are not misled into believing that you are being victimized by an individual extorting exorbitant profits from trusting clients. Certainly, you should be fully cognizant to the realities of business life when negotiating with others for services and/or products. But at the same time, take whatever steps are necessary, such as getting a number of quotes or bids, to enable you to determine the market price for the kind of services you seek. An understanding of what costs are, in the technical sense, also helps.

THE COST OF DOING BUSINESS

It is possible that you already have a complete understanding of entrepreneurial and business costs of all kinds. However, my experience in conducting seminars is that a surprisingly large number of executives have a great interest in any information regarding the costs of doing business, and so are interested in even refreshers on the subject. In that spirit, the following basic explanations are offered.

What Are Costs?

For accounting purposes, there are two broad categories of costs *direct* and *indirect*. These require definition.

Direct costs are costs incurred specifically for a given contract or project. In consulting, they would normally be labor costs, because consulting is principally a service and so is usually labor intensive. However, there could be some miscellaneous costs that are sizeable enough to be billed directly to the client or the project. These might include travel and related expense, printing or duplicating reports, postage, telephone tolls, special services, and other such items. Such costs, if they are directly attributable to the project and therefore assigned as direct cost, would either be billed directly to the client or be assigned as part of the project cost, depending on how the contract is written. That is, they would appear on your bill as separate items if the agreement you have with your consultants calls for hourly or daily rates plus expenses. But if you have asked for a fixed price—a total price for the project—the consultant would normally have estimated all such extra costs and included them in his or her fixed price for the job. They would still be direct cost, but would be billed to the project as a whole, so you would not perceive them as a separate item.

Indirect costs, on the other hand, are costs that cannot be identified specifically as incurred directly in support of some given contract or project. Basic telephone charges, rent, heat, light, insurance, taxes, and so forth are examples of indirect costs. These are real costs, but there is no way to establish precisely how much of a rent or mortgage payment went into some specific program, and so they are indirect and must be recovered in some other manner than as direct billing to the project. Usually they are charged as overhead or some other indirect category.

In any case, the principle that a business must recover *all* costs if it is to survive is immutable. It is essential to understand that and to bear it in mind in exploring the consultant's business realities.

Professional accountants subdivide and subclassify direct and indirect costs in many ways. That is necessary for good accounting practice and good management, especially for large and complex organizations. But only the broad categories will be dealt with here because it is only the *principles* that are of interest for the purposes of this discussion.

Consulting Fees and Related Costs

There are many ways in which consultants structure their fees depending on the nature of what they do, their personal preferences and biases, the accepted or standard practices in their technical and professional specialties, and sundry other factors. The basic categories for fee setting are daily rates, hourly rates (usually with schedules for overtime, weekends, holidays, etc.), and fixed or for-the-job prices.

As a rule, the consultant who is charging you on the basis of hourly or daily fees is expressing that rate as the total labor charge for his or her service, but that does not include extraordinary expenses. If the consultant must travel a great enough distance (over 50 miles) in your behalf to require overnight lodging, travel and per diem expenses are added to the daily or hourly rate. Those expenses include lodging and meals.

Governments normally allot some fixed per diem expense for lodging and meals, plus travel at coach or tourist rates. Private-sector companies may be more or less generous. One common practice is to charge actual rates, whatever they are, as long as they are whatever is considered reasonable. In some cases the consultant may ask you to furnish air tickets and have lodging billed directly to you. The consultant then bills you only for minor items of travel and subsistence. The entire matter is usually negotiable, but it ought to be agreed upon in advance to avoid problems that can easily arise if a clear understanding has not been established. If your organization has a firm, fixed policy about what costs and rates are allowable, for example, it is in your direct interest to make the provisions of this policy clear to your consultant and be sure that the two of you are agreed on what the expense reimbursement will be or at least what the set limits are.

On the other hand, your consultant may have some fixed policies of his or her own, and it is necessary that these be made known to you to prevent later conflict. In my own case, partly due to the nature of the requirements and conditions of my consulting specialties and partly due to my own distaste for meticulous, detailed, and (in my biased opinion) unnecessary recordkeeping, I prefer to charge a flat daily rate, without provision for premium-time charges. That is, my daily rate is the same for an 8-hour day as it is for a 14-hour day (a not unusual day in the maelstrom of a major proposal effort), and it is the same for Tuesday or Thursday as for Saturday and Sunday—or for a holiday, for that matter. I accommodate this by charging a daily rate that is calculated carefully to compensate me for the frequent long days, and I take pains to make sure that my client understands this.

It is quite possible that I am in the minority of consultants in this respect. Probably a majority charge by the hour or for a distinct 8-hour day and then charge premium rates for overtime, weekends, and holidays worked. That is their prerogative, but it is your prerogative to ask questions and make sure you understand the consultant's position in this matter of rates.

FOR-THE-JOB PRICING

Of course, it is possible that you may never have occasion to retain a consultant on the basis of a day rate. Many consulting projects are carried out on the basis of flat, for-the-job prices. You issue a request for proposals, evaluate responses, and negotiate a contract on the basis of the proposed costs and the final negotiated figures. Here, the question is a different one, for day rates often do not enter the picture at all. You are faced, instead, with a total price for the job, and you are not able to judge what portion of the price is actually cost and what portion is profit. It can be more difficult to judge the reasonableness of this type of cost proposal.

HELP FROM OTHER MODELS

Once again, the practices of government agencies and large corporations offer models. The government practice is usually to call for a flat, for-the-job price for only relatively small projects, those not larger than that authorized by the Small Purchases Act as a ceiling (currently $25,000). However, any agency's contracting official may set the ceiling lower than that, and many do. A different approach is employed for larger projects, requiring detailed disclosure of the elements entering into the final quotation. That helps the client in judging whether the final, bottom-line price is reasonable.

Typically, such standards of the federal government and others who mandate the provision of detailed cost analyses include requirements for separate disclosure of direct and indirect cost centers along the following lines:

- Direct labor rates of each class and category of labor, with estimates of the number of hours required of each class and category.
- Overhead rate and extensions of each labor category, per direct-labor hours and rates, into actual dollars.
- Other direct costs to be charged to the project such as travel, printing, and telephone tolls.
- Other burdens such as general and administrative (G & A) rates, and their extensions into dollars.
- Additional labor on a consulting basis—rates, time, and dollars.
- Fee or profit rate and/or actual dollars.

It is considerably easier to judge the reasonableness of proposed charges when they are presented in this way and thus are subject to analyses and comparisons with whatever standards are available.

G & A RATES

G & A rates cover burden or indirect rates that are not properly part of the overhead. They are more difficult to generalize about than the others because they vary more. In many cases, they are quite small—2 to 5 percent—while in others they may run as high as 30 percent. Often it is necessary to examine the entire cost pool to make a judgment.

COMPARISONS AND JUDGMENTS

It is generally accepted that a manufacturing enterprise that is *capital intensive* (i.e., it has a great deal of money invested in equipment and inventory as the chief basis for the enterprise) may have as large an overhead rate as 400 percent, or four times its direct costs for turning out the products. On the other hand, *labor-intensive* enterprises, such as consulting, tend to have much lower overhead rates. Many operate at as little as 40 to 50 percent, and few service or other labor-intensive enterprises require more than 100 to 125 percent to function. In fact, contracting officials in government tend to view those service enterprises quoting overhead rates at 100 percent or more to be costly contractors and probably not very efficiently managed.

Those are probably reasonable mileposts to observe in judging costs when you have required a detailed breakdown. Such a breakdown affords you a view of several cost areas in which you can judge whether the rates are competitive with whatever the market is or should be.

For example, you can easily judge whether it is reasonable to pay a typist $25 an hour or a computer programmer $75 an hour, and you can judge whether a 265-percent overhead rate is defensible.

COST POOLS

When a large contract is at stake, and especially when the contract is to be cost-reimbursable, as a client you can in good conscience request a complete cost-pool presentation to support the consultant's claimed burden rates. That is, you can require the consultant to furnish a complete accounting of all costs that are part of the overhead pool, the G & A pool, if one is claimed, and fringe benefits. (Some organizations include costs for fringe benefits in the overhead pool, while others collect those costs in a separate fringe benefits pool.) Of course, the consultant must also furnish figures on gross sales and total direct labor so that the ratios of indirect to direct costs that represent the rates can be verified.

Government agencies often demand such complete financial and accounting disclosures when a large contract is at stake and especially when the contract is to be a cost-plus or other reimbursable type. The idea behind this is to require the proposer to document both the direct costs and the burden rates claimed, especially when the proposer cannot offer certified overhead and G & A rates (i.e., rates that have been verified in some way, as by audit). Such analyses and disclosures also furnish government contracting officials a basis and much useful data for negotiations.

Many consultants are reluctant to furnish such detailed information; it is one reason why many organizations choose not to seek government business. But even those who do make such disclosures to government agencies may decline to do so to private-sector organizations. That is, you may or may not be successful in persuading consultants to disclose such detailed financial information. However, you probably do not need this much cost detail to protect yourself against gouging and to glean enough information for negotiations. The pressure of competition, your knowledge of the normal market for the services, and your skill in negotiating are normally enough to ensure reasonable prices if you bear some of the following basic factors in mind.

FACTORS AFFECTING BURDEN RATES

You must consider the factors that affect the burden rates. One major element of overhead, for example, is the cost of rent or mortgage payments on the work space. But there are many other costs associated with supporting staff employees, whether one or many. There are the costs of telephone service, office supplies, office furniture and equipment (desks, typewriters, desktop computers, copiers, etc.), and many related facilities such as employee parking spaces.

All of these costs are valid, and the consultant contractor, whether an individual or a company, is entitled to include a fair share of them in billing the client. However, the nature of consulting work is such that in many cases the bulk of the work is performed on the client's premises—*your* premises—and you provide all or nearly all the heat, light, desks, copiers, office supplies, and other such support required to get the job done.

In return for this support at your expense, you are entitled to some reduction in the overhead rate charged, and this is a legitimate cost to make the subject of negotiation. This is an excellent reason to want to see what the consultant's burden rates are—what they are normally and what concessions are made to you when the work is to be done on your premises. Of course, the consultant's overhead does not go to zero because the work is performed primarily or even completely on your premises, but it must logically be reduced by some amount, perhaps 5 or 10 percent. In any case, you are entitled to pursue such a reduction in the cost negotiations.

HOW MUCH PROFIT?

In the fixed-price contract you have no way of knowing what the consultant's net profit is or, indeed, whether the job has produced a profit at all. However, in cases in which the consultant must present a complete cost analysis, the nominal fee or profit is listed—nominal, because it is part of the estimate. Even then you do not know what the actual fee or profit is, but you do know what the consultant's notion of a proper fee or profit is.

Morally, the contractor is always entitled to a profit that is in some proportion to the risk taken. A high-risk project entitles the consultant to shoot for a larger profit than in the case of a low-risk job such as a cost-reimbursable contract.

Here again, full disclosure of cost estimates offers you some assistance in judging the reasonableness of the costs. As to what fees and profits ought to be today, I suggest approximately 10 to 12 percent for low-risk projects and 15 to 20 percent for high-risk projects.

THE INDEPENDENT CONSULTANT VERSUS THE ORGANIZATION

One major concern many clients have in contracting for expert services is the decision as to whether to contract with an individual, independent consultant or with a consultant organization. The differences between them may well represent a substantial difference in cost to you. Here are some relevant factors to consider.

The consulting organization is likely to have a lower overhead than is the independent consultant because the organization has a larger labor base over which to spread indirect costs. However, this is offset slightly by the tendency of larger organizations to provide larger and more comprehensive benefits packages than independent consultants afford themselves, by more expensive suites of offices, and by other factors. Therefore, the large organization may, in the end, have a higher overhead than the independent practitioner. That is one reason you should require disclosure of direct and indirect rates on larger contracts. You may be surprised by these disclosures, but they are likely to reveal which is truly the lower-cost producer.

Independent consultants probably pay themselves larger salaries than large organizations pay their staff consultants, but large organizations tend to mark up staff salaries substantially in setting billing rates, so they do not necessarily offer you a saving.

The organization may provide the resumés of its most highly qualified experts and is likely to base its cost estimates on these figures, but you may or may not find these experts actually working on your project after you have awarded them the contract and agreed to the costs based on their salaries. As a rule, you have no assurance that the organization will provide these individuals unless you take special measures. The contractor will normally reserve the right to assign whoever is readily available at the time, and those assigned may be relatively junior people. However, you can make it a condition of the contract that the proposer must supply the individuals named or others of equal qualification. And you may reserve to yourself the right to approve or disapprove of any substitute personnel. It is normally a wise move to make when contracting with a large consulting organization.

Ordinarily, you do not have this problem when dealing with an independent consultant. However, it can happen even then (independent consultants may have associates and not handle all projects personally), and it may prove wise to insist on the right to approve anyone assigned to the job even when you are contracting with independent consultants.

Chapter Nine

Establishing and Maintaining Good Working Relationships

Each party to an agreement expects something of the other. That is as it should be: A clear understanding is necessary to an effective working relationship. But it is necessary to have a clear understanding both of what the consultant has agreed specifically to provide and of what you may reasonably expect, whether specified or not.

MAKING IT HAPPEN

It is possible to accomplish what you set out to accomplish without warmth or cordiality between you and your consultant, but better results are almost surely achieved when the working relationship is a friendly one. Truly good working relationships do not often emerge automatically or naturally; they must be made to happen. Here, as in most things, Murphy's Law is hard at work on a full-time basis: "Anything that can go wrong will." Yet, it is not difficult to make a good working relationship happen.

There are so many aspects to establishing and maintaining a good working relationship that a discussion of them tends to range widely; thus, a rather diverse set of topics will appear in this chapter. Since mutual respect for each other is an excellent starting point for client–consultant working relationships, that will be discussed first. Respect stems from an understanding of each other, not necessarily as individuals but as practitioners of and in whatever roles we play.

A SENSITIVITY ISSUE

Many consultants are sensitive about how consultants in general are regarded in the professional and business worlds. That sensitivity is not entirely without basis: The consulting profession has been and often is maligned. That is not always unjustified, of course; consultants vary in their competence, as most humans do. But the derogation of consultants generally is often unjust, and resulting from unsatisfactory performances that are not the fault of the consultants. This is not a condemnation of clients generally, although client shortcomings such as failure to disclose necessary information or inaccurate explanation of problems and needs—have sometimes been the cause of problems. A frequent cause of unsatisfactory consulting services is much simpler to explain: Clients often retain the *wrong* consultants for their needs by assuming that any consultant within what appears to be the appropriate field will be satisfactory or by failing to get a full understanding of their own needs before attempting to find and select a consultant.

Choice of the wrong consultant often arises from the client's mistaken belief in the infallibility of consultants of some given general description—that a doctor is a doctor is a doctor, for example, and that every doctor is an expert in all medical matters. The fact is that medicine and a great many other fields (e.g., electronics and marketing) have grown so widely and so diversely that it now is impossible for anyone to know it all, and specialists must specialize in some narrow area of their field if they are to be truly specialized. The words *specialist* and *specialty* have quite different connotations today than they had only a few years ago, in that specialties tend to be far narrower today, as the knowledge within each field broadens. Therefore, one step toward achieving better working relationships is to take pains to see to it that you have properly identified your needs and retained the right consultant for the job.

THE ROLES CONSULTANTS AND CLIENTS PLAY

Everyone plays many roles in life: father, mother, teacher, jailer, disciplinarian, guardian, executive, expert, supporter, attacker, employer, employee, benevolent dictator, not-so-benevolent dictator, critic, and others. A number of the roles are played in homes and others in offices. Some people play still other roles in associations, churches, synagogues, PTA, civic groups, and other groups to which they belong. Some of these roles are played by deliberate choice; others are established solely in others' views or as the inevitable result of their positions vis-à-vis the position of the role-player. If you are an editor, for example, the writers whose work you edit cannot help but regard you as a critic, although you may regard yourself as the writer's helper and alter ego. Others in the organization are likely to see you in still another light.

That is as fundamental a truth for consultants in their professional roles as it is for others. Consultants tend to perceive themselves as contractors, suppliers of professional services. Clients, however, often tend to view consultants as subordinates, especially when the consultants work primarily on the clients' premises. That is an understandable view when a consultant is actually retained as a technical or professional temporary, brought on board primarily to augment the in-house staff for a short time. But when the consultant is retained to supply knowledge and/or skills not otherwise available in house, the perspective should be quite different, and client–consultant relationships will usually benefit from viewing the consultant as an associate or contractor of equal standing.

In short, the client and consultant ought to be peers, able to exchange information and ideas on a more or less equal basis, despite the natural tendency of any contractor to indulge a client as much as possible. But with an employer–employee relationship established, even if it is an illusory one, the openness and honesty of communication is compromised severely. The meaning of the term *client* is important here, for the consultant you retain may or may not work directly with you or with any executive; the consultant may be required by the nature of the job to work with employees below executive and managerial levels. In that case, that term *client* refers to any and all employees with whom the consultant must work, and that sometimes leads to problems.

The federal government is conscious of this problem and is also sensitive to the attitudes of labor unions of government employees. The regulations concerning the relationships between government employees and contractor employees are therefore quite specific in trying to prevent problems. They provide that contractors, especially those working on government premises, must not be given orders by federal employees, nor can the contractors direct the employees of the government. The two can exchange technical information—suggestions, ideas, explanations of requirements, and the like—but cannot issue to one another anything resembling orders.

CONSULTING IS A BUSINESS

It is important to recognize that consulting is a business, as well as a profession, and the consultant is subject to all the risks and hazards of any business enterprise. Hardheaded—that is, thoroughly practical—business considerations must drive the consulting profession if consultants are to survive and be able to provide their services to clients. In fact, a consulting practice is an entrepreneurial venture. If you have not thought of a consultant as an entrepreneur, it is time to recognize this and understand it. You must also understand all of its implications if you are to develop a good working relationship with the consultant.

A great deal of difficulty arises from what many perceive as exorbitant rates charged by consultants. Clients are often unable to understand why consultants charge $500 to $1,000 or even more per day for their services, especially when they work from their homes and supposedly have no expenses. Is this not outrageous? Does this not add up to $125,000 to $250,000 or more per year? Is that not rather high for a consultant?

It would be high, perhaps too high, if the consultant were fortunate enough to work every day of the week and every week of the year at the normal daily rate and truly had no expenses. Of course, that is not the case at all. Few consultants are fortunate enough to work more than two-thirds of the hours and days they have available (many would work for far lower rates if that were the case), and they do have many *other* expenses. Idle or unbilled time is an expense for professionals, chargeable only to overhead activities, such as marketing and administration. Even if they have offices in their own homes, they have telephones, advertising, postage, office equipment, marketing, and many other expenses.

One reason clients sometimes consider consultants' rates to be too high is that they misunderstand the consultant's role. I was once summoned to a prospective client's office to discuss writing a proposal. The is one of the services I provide, based on my extensive knowledge of the field. However, this prospective client appeared to be on the verge of fainting when I quoted my daily rate. She fairly screamed, "That's pretty expensive for a writer!"

I tried in vain to explain that the writing was incidental, despite its importance, and that my fee was for my services and advice as an expert in the field, with a track record of having won several hundred million dollars in contracts for past employers and clients. It was to no avail; the client stubbornly refused to perceive a difference between a marketing consultant who delivered his marketing guidance by actually writing proposals and a writer who wrote proposals. I was compelled to admit defeat.

If the consultant succeeds in achieving about 175 billable days in the year at $500, gross revenue is $87,500. Given a modest and typical overhead rate of 50 percent (and many consulting firms struggle mightily and often unsuccessfully to keep their overhead rate below 100 percent), indirect expenses represent $43,750. That permits the consultant to pay himself or herself a maximum of $43,750, which would leave zero profit for the enterprise. To realize even a minimal 5 percent profit, the consultant must not draw more than $40,000 a year, hardly a munificent sum for the labor and risks of an independent venture.

The items that make up overhead or indirect costs fall into more than one broad class for the consultant, just as they do for any other business:

Rent, light, heat, telephone, and other utilities
Office furniture and equipment
Office supplies
Advertising
Insurance and taxes
Indirect labor
Losses

The last two items may require just a little explanation. If the consultant operates the venture on a strictly business basis, the consulting practice is an entity and the consultant is a salaried employee as well as the proprietor or chief stockholder. As such, the consultant is paid a salary by the business entity. Let us say, for illustration, that in this case it is $40,000. That is, whether the consultant is working hours billed to a client, taking a day off, making marketing calls, working on the books, writing a brochure, or doing anything else, he or she is being paid. That is, the consultant's salary is one of the *costs*, probably the principal cost, of the venture. It is as much a cost as are rent, advertising, and taxes. Profit—net profit, that is—is what (if anything) is left after *all costs*, including taxes and salaries. That is the reality with which the consultant is faced every day, and it must be taken into account in calculating the fees and rates the consultant must charge clients to survive.

Although probably no area offers as great a potential for disagreements and disputes as do the various areas of costs, the problem can be minimized with understanding of the realities. However, all areas represent potential opportunities for such disputes unless suitable measures are taken in advance to prevent the problems from arising.

The same considerations apply to expenses. Some consultants prefer to charge a flat per diem rate for subsistence, plus travel costs, while others are content to bill for and recover actual rates. But they may resist having any ceiling imposed. They may think they are entitled to the privilege of traveling first class and being reimbursed for first-class accommodations on airlines, in hotels, and elsewhere, whereas client policy (and perhaps the IRS) think otherwise. You can see the potential for problems here, if the agreement is not clearly established up front.

I pursue what is probably an unusual fee-setting policy: I charge a flat daily rate without regard to how many hours are in the day or what day of the week or year it is; I never charge premiums for holidays, or overtime because I wish to keep life as simple as possible. That philosophy results in a curious paradox. I charge an apparently lower rate by the hour than I do by the day. That is, if you were to divide my daily rate by 8, the nominal workday hours, you would find a result considerably larger than the hourly rate I quote on the few occasions when someone wishes to engage my services for only a few hours. This is easily explained: My hourly rate is firm, and the client must pay me that rate for *each and every hour* under an hourly-rate arrangement, unlike the daily-rate arrangement. I am careful to explain this when clients are appraising what I ask to estimate the total cost and decide on the better rate or fee schedule to pursue.

BUT CONSULTING IS ALSO A PROFESSION

Consultants like to think that consulting is a profession and that they are professionals. But the question of whether consultants are professionals is more than a matter of individual sensitivity and pride; it has a much more practical side to it. It is important to good working relationships that clients and prospective clients grant consultants recognition as professionals because it is an integral part of their self-image and thus is important to them. When Abraham Lincoln observed that a lawyer's time and knowledge were what he had as his stock in trade, it is likely that he had not heard the term *consultant*, but he would probably have included that class of service specialists had he known of them, for the parallel is close.

The term *professional* is not easily defined, and it has been the subject of many vigorous discussions and disputes. The term exists largely in the mind—in the concepts and interpretations of the practitioners in trades and skills who required extensive formal education and, usually, some kind of board certification. Not all consultants fit this standard, if it is a standard, but the functions of consultants are quite similar to those of lawyers, physicians, and others in that the work involves advising and related activities based on special knowledge and skills.

At the same time, the more thoughtful among the consulting profession also recognize the anomaly, the valid argument that consulting is not itself a profession, but is simply the way some *practice* their professions, even when the work they do is normally considered a professional calling. For example, a police offical would not normally be considered a professional, and yet retired police officers and officials often become consultants on security to private-sector organizations.

The anomaly aside, what is probably most important in the client–consultant relationship is that the consultant, like the physician and the lawyer, must have the confidence and trust of the client to function effectively. In fact, for greatest effectiveness the confidence and trust must be mutual between consultant and client. Each must approach the working relationship with dignity and honesty.

PLAYING FAIR

Nothing is quite so destructive of a good working relationship with a contractor as the suspicion that you are not playing fair with him or her. Note the use of the word *suspicion*, for it is the mere suspicion, even when it is unjustified, that does the damage. For example, I have known unscrupulous clients to use a consultant's unsolicited proposal as an inspiration to invite competitive proposals. That is unfair if the consultant is offering services based on his or her proprietary ideas and is offering them to you in confidence. The fact that you did not ask for the proposal is not itself grounds for considering its contents to be proprietary, but when they are—and it should normally be easy enough to judge that—you should not then invite others to propose their own versions of the service offered. (Unfortunately, this kind of unethical behavior is exhibited occasionally, and it accounts in part for the reluctance of many consultants to reveal anything until they are under contract.)

Honesty ought to be an inherent element of professionalism. Certainly, it is essential for a healthy and productive working relationship between you and your consultant. But the definition of honesty is far from absolute. Quite the contrary, it is a relative term.

Most people tend to use the word *honesty* rather carelessly, on the assumption that there is general agreement on the meaning of the word. It rarely occurs to people that in practice honesty is a relative quality. For example, when you see Aunt Tillie in her new summer outfit, which you regard as in execrably bad taste, you say, "Oh, Auntie, you look so *good* in that beautiful outfit!" That's a white lie, an excusable bit of dishonesty committed in the interest of courtesy and kindness. And if the boss shows up at work one day with a garish necktie and solicits your opinion about it, you are going to tell a white lie in the interest of diplomacy and good sense—in the interest of self-preservation.

Because of these kinds of considerations, especially the latter one, when you explain to your consultant the clever system you, your superiors, or some other consultant designed for your organization, the consultant is going to be reluctant to be critical, even if you specifically solicit his or her opinion of the system. That would be fine if the consultant truly approved of your system; he or she could honestly endorse it. But what if the consultant perceived weaknesses and faults in the system? That is another story: Being honest in this case might be suicidal, so you might not be told what you consultant really thinks.

It works the other way too. You, as the client, might find it difficult to be entirely frank with your consultant. In some circumstances, a frank answer might require you to be critical of your superior or your company. It might even require you to confess a failure on your own part. You would understandably shy away from a totally honest answer in these circumstances.

THE BABEL OF MODERN JARGON

The legal profession, like the medical one, has long been given to the use of obscure Latin phrases that few outside the profession understand. Even if the terms are translated they are difficult to understand. *Habeas corpus*, for example, literally means that "you have the body" or "deliver the body." But in practice it means that a court appearance and judgment are required. Even more misunderstood is the legal term *corpus delicti*, which many misinterpret as meaning that the body of the victim must be found to prove murder, whereas the true meaning refers to proving that the crime was committed—to the "body" of the crime, that is. Modern psychologists often refer to changing behavior as an important objective of what they do, but the word *behavior* has a special meaning, which is not *deportment*, as many laypeople mistakenly believe. The word is used in a clinical sense. When, as a writer-developer of training systems, I explained in plain, layperson's terms this special meaning and significance of the word *behavior*, I found myself under attack for "giving the store away" by letting the layperson know what psychologists and training specialists were talking about—that is, giving away what they sold! (Even more upsetting, however, was the discovery that some of these very specialists did not themselves understand the true meaning of the term, but had merely learned to parrot the language of their more thoughtful peers. They, too, thought that *behavior* referred to deportment, and they complained about the use of the lay terms in place of their professional jargon in my introductory write-up.)

The use of highly technical and usually obscure jargon grows up as part of the professional mystique, and it comes to be taken for granted as a necessary part of the professional image. It may or may not be intended to deceive or to conceal truth, but all too often that is its effect. Unfortunately, in many cases it is employed to impress a client and supposedly prove the worth of a highly technical, highly specialized consultant. But even that is not always the case. I have encountered consultants who had learned somehow to use the mystical jargon of their professions without truly understanding it. They were content to establish an image that others would accept as one of professional competence, thus affording them entrée to their chosen field.

Fortunately, although it is not uncommon, this is not the usual case. Jargon does have a legitimate function when it is used within the circle of professionals in the field, for it is a convenient shorthand that contributes to efficiency of communication *within the field.* When an electronics engineer explains that what he or she is doing is necessary to get the signal "out of the grass," another experienced engineer understands that the engineer is trying to improve the signal-to-noise ratio because the background noise is smothering the signal. This probably would have no significance to you, as a layperson, yet you might have to understand the significance of the remark; hence, you need to have this technical jargon put into everyday English.

This is understandable. The evil arises when the specialist deliberately confuses and deceives the layperson by offering jargon as explanation. Sometimes the consultant specialist who does so knows very well that clients are often reluctant to admit to not having the faintest idea what such terms mean. However, it is much more often the case that the consultant is sincere and well-intentioned but completely unaware that he or she has failed to communicate with the client.

What to Do About It

Some consultants and other experts use mystifying jargon deliberately, expecting to achieve a certain effect. But they are mistaken to believe that the use of cryptic jargon is appropriate or even necessary to their professional image. Quite the contrary, it much more in keeping with consulting professionalism to do whatever is necessary to ensure that the client gains a full and complete understanding of the consultant's work through reports, presentations, and/or other means. It is, in fact, a mistake for you, the client, to permit misunderstanding or lack of understanding to happen. You should not be expected to understand the special jargon and technical terms of the consultant's special field; you are completely entitled to and should demand to have everything explained—*reported,* that is—in simple, lay language. You should ask as many questions as necessary to make your understanding thorough and complete. If the report is a written one, as it usually is in a sizeable project (with or without ancillary verbal presentations), you have the right and perhaps even the obligation to require that it be submitted to you in draft format for review, criticism, and suggestions before it is made final and committed for the record.

Chapter Ten

Common Problems and How to Avoid or Solve Them

The most worrisome projects are those in which there are apparently no problems, for experience teaches us to expect the unexpected when it comes to problems.

THE MOST COMMON PROBLEMS ARE THE UNCOMMON PROBLEMS

Despite your best efforts to maintain an excellent working relationship with your consultant, problems will arise—some in connection with that working relationship, others totally unconnected with it—because problems are a way of life in the business world.

It is important to recognize that despite the best planning, the unexpected will happen again and again. It is most unlikely that you or your consultant will foresee all possible calamities and disappointments, but if you cannot predict and anticipate each problem, you can predict and anticipate that there will almost certainly *be* problems. They can be especially exasperating because so often it is that which you thought most predictable and dependable that fails!

For example, when I was helping a company that manufactures computer printers prepare a proposal for an important contract, the company's marketing director and I were working all through the night before the proposal had to be delivered—in an unfortunately typical crisis—when the printer failed us. With the plant and all the other offices closed and neither of us especially expert in using, much less maintaining, printers, we would have been in a panic had we not had a second printer standing by and available for immediate use. (We also had a backup computer and word processor available.) Contingency planning ought to be a standard part of preparation to begin a project. Make it a rule that for any and every function that is not under your direct control you have a contingency plan. For example, when the printer who normally did the printing for our company balked at promising to print our four-volume proposal on the schedule we required, we had a standby print shop ready to handle the job. When our regular printer learned this, he hastily revised his schedules and handled the job for us after all. So often, it is the mere fact of having the alternative plan that enables you to avoid using it.

Always develop and detail your plans to the extent that you can define every important task and subtask. Then identify those in which you are dependent on someone else—even another individual or department in your own organization. (Unfortunately, heads of other departments sometimes behave as though they were rivals, rather than associates.) Prepare a fallback plan (some people refer to it as "Plan B") for each of these tasks per the format shown in Figure 10–1. It can be your lifeline in many cases.

Enlist the help of your consultant in developing these detailed plans and identifying all the tasks and subtasks. Unfortunately, clients often fail to make adequate use of consulting help in their planning. In fact, when you have requested proposals from contenders for your project, you should require them to make up a list of tasks and subtasks in their proposals, with their own proposed methods for accomplishing each task. You can then easily convert this to your own needs for planning and managing the project with Plans A and B.

BE SURE YOU IDENTIFY THE *ENTIRE* REQUIREMENT IN ADVANCE

Along these same lines is the need to anticipate just what it is you need from your consultant. Presumably, you need the consultant's technical skills and services, but just what are those services? Are they confined to advising you? Performing some task or tasks? Training your staff? Or is there something more?

It is that "something more" that can cause you to come to grief if you have not thought your needs out thoroughly in advance. Suppose, for example, that making a stand-up verbal presentation of the project to an assemblage in your company is an important element of the project, but you do not wish to make

TASK/SUBTASK	PLAN A	PLAN B
Designing program		
* Study and survey	Wiggins/ Computer dept	Hirsch/consultant
* Programming	Kelly/Computer dept	Earle/consultant
* Testing	Jones/Computer dept	Harrison/consultant
Writing computer-support section	Hagan/Computer dept	Jones and Weiss Co.
Printing proposal	Offset-Litho Co.	Tiny Printers, Inc.

Figure 10–1. Sample Fallback Plan.

that presentation personally. Perhaps you shrink from public speaking, fear that you will not know enough technically to handle all the questions, or for some other reason want your consultant to make the presentation. But suppose that your consultant is also reluctant to make formal presentations or, although willing to do so, is quite poor at this art. The same thing applies to other requirements of the project, such as writing a lengthy report or manual about the program or training others in it. Clients often want consultant contractors to handle those tasks, and, in fact, they may be the most important part of the project. But, again, suppose your consultant is simply not an effective writer or trainer?

At this point there is not a great deal you can do about the problem. You must somehow undertake to do it yourself, tolerate whatever job your consultant can make of it, or seek another consultant to come in for a crash study and fill-in, not a desirable prospect.

This goes back to matters discussed in earlier chapters: identifying and defining your needs—that is, determining precisely what it is you want your consultant to do and using that as a guideline in selecting the consultant. Once again, it is a matter of careful and thorough advance planning. You want to make sure that your consultant can do *all* the tasks you want done, including making formal stand-up presentations to large groups, writing suitable articles and reports, lecturing, and whatever else you perceive as a requirement.

PERSONALITY CONFLICTS AND OTHER PROBLEMS OF CONSULTING

The problems discussed so far are general ones that might be described as technical or program difficulties, problems that might occur in any project. However, there is another set of problems—some of them rather distasteful—that sometimes arise in consulting situations.

Unfortunately, consulting sometimes takes on an adversarial aspect, especially in situations in which the consultant works on the client's premises as a kind of professional temporary, doing much the same kind of work the regular staff workers do. It is here, in the relationship between the consultant and the staff employees, that the client-consultant relationship most often runs into problems.

The consultant and the individual who made the decision to retain the consultant normally have a mutual goal: the successful accomplishment of the mission in the most effective and efficient manner possible. But that mutuality of interest—or, to be more precise, that *perception* of mutual interest—does not necessarily carry over to the consultant's relationship with staff employees assigned to the work. Unfortunately, staff members often regard the consultant with a great deal of hostility, based on assumptions that are usually false. Once again, it is necessary to deal with individuals' perceptions. When a consultant is brought in to work beside the regular employees in an organization, they often tend to regard the consultant as a threat as well as an affront, someone whose interests are anything but identical with theirs.

The threat is perceived because employees tend to believe

that the reason for bringing a consultant in is because management lacks confidence in the regular staff. In this frame of reference, the presence of the consultant is a direct affront.

The consultant may become even more fiercely resented when employees learn that the consultant earns considerably more than they do. They ignore the fact that the consultant gets no fringe benefits, has no job security, and bears the burden of many business expenses.

Finally, if employees learn that the consultant can carry out certain chores they do not have, the resentment may become even more fierce, as my own experience taught me on one of my early consulting assignments.

I was one of six consultant specialists in technical writing called in to help a major computer manufacturer get out of difficulties. The manufacturer had sold a custom-made mainframe computer to the U.S. Navy, but the Navy had rejected the manuals provided and had withheld payment until satisfactory manuals were delivered.

We discovered that the publications department was staffed with experienced writers whose technical knowledge of computers was rather scant, and that was reflected in the manuals they had prepared. They normally wrote manuals for the lay user and were not at all familiar with military documentation standards and requirements. They had had great difficulty in interpreting and translating the heavy engineering data into complete and effective how-to-do-it instructions for computer operators, programmers, and maintenance technicians.

The staff writers were humiliated by the Navy's rejection of their work, and possibly even a bit guilt-ridden because they did not have the necessary technical knowledge or knowledge of military manuals. In any case, their resentment of us and their hostility to us was evident immediately. For example, after I reviewed some basic data relevant to the manual assigned to me for review and first aid, I asked one of the senior writers on the staff a question about some of the technical data that I found unclear. (At this point, I did not yet know that these writers were journalism and communications majors who had not had any engineering training.) The response was a somewhat evasive admission that he did not know the answer. I then recognized the problem and asked—in all innocence and quite sincerely—to whom he would refer me for technical information. To my surprise, he flared up in anger and indignantly demanded to known whether I was implying that he did not know what he was doing or was incompetent in some way.

Of course, that was a revelation. I stammered an embarrassed apology, unsure of what offense I was apologizing for, and withdrew puzzled and a bit hurt that my well-intentioned query was so misunderstood. I had certainly not been sneering, nor had I intended to be offensive in any way. Months later that gentleman apologized to me for his outburst. But that was only after many weeks of quiet diplomacy on my part and his hard-won recognition that we were being helpful, that they were learning a great deal about preparing manuals for the military, and that there was no evil intent on our part or on the part of their own management to derogate their capabilities and contributions.

On another occasion, not long after this incident and while I was still learning how to handle myself on clients' premises in awkward situations, I was working in New York on an assignment to write manuals for another major computer manufacturer. I was selected by the executive in charge of the company's publications to write the lead manual because I had had considerable general, as well as technical and military, writing experience. A lower-level supervisor was assigned to organize the complement of consultant writers, of whom there were about 30. His first requirement was that I write an outline describing how I proposed to handle my assignment and deposit it on his desk by noon.

I met his deadline, but before the afternoon was over he

returned to my desk, flung the outline down—thoroughly marked up and scribbled over—and advised me that *that* was how he wanted it done.

I demurred, explaining that I believed the way I proposed to do the job was the right way. He ignored my plea and insisted that if I was going to work there I was going to do what he wanted, not what I wanted. I thereupon yielded.

It was a serious mistake. Later, when the executive in charge reviewed my draft manuscript, he expressed his disappointment. I explained what had happened and showed him the original outline. He agreed that I had been right in my approach but wrong in yielding. He said that I should have had too much professional integrity to take what I knew was the wrong approach to the job and should have consulted him about the difference of opinion.

He was absolutely right, of course. I was thoroughly ashamed that I had been so timid, and it was a lesson that remained with me from that day forward.

These are common problems in client-consultant relationships, but they are not inevitable or unavoidable. Inasmuch as I was able finally to establish a cordial working relationship with the employees in the first case cited, it demonstrates that such hostility is not necessarily an automatic response. As for the second case, I should have taken the matter up with the executive who had hired me. He was my client, he had interviewed me originally for the assignment, and he had trusted my judgment, a trust I had not served well.

These problems can usually be avoided or at least minimized with the following procedures:

1. Consultants working on your premises should refrain from discussing their work and their earnings with your employees. It would probably be helpful to discuss this with con-

sultants you retain and explain why you request observance of such a policy.

2. Consultants must be diplomatic. If consultants will be working with or alongside your regular employees, especially on a long-term basis, interview them with a view to assessing their personalities and views. You want quiet individuals who get along, do not "come on strongly," dress conservatively, and speak softly. You might also check on personality traits when you check references.
3. You also want consultants who have integrity, who will not permit themselves to be bullied into failing on the job or doing a job badly. Explain that you do not want your consultants to get into quarrels with any of your employees, but to come and discuss problems with you, if any arise.
4. Bear all these points in mind (you might want to prepare a checklist) when you verify references with consultants' other clients. (Do ask consultants to furnish such references.)

Despite all my earlier exhortations to plan carefully and define everything in advance and in great detail, I must admit that is an ideal that is not always attainable. Often it is not possible to set forth all the details in advance, but only make a start and develop plans as you proceed.

For example, I recently spent a week in San Antonio assisting a small company in writing a proposal. The client had called me 10 days earlier to determine whether I would be available, and had explained the job briefly. Now he called on Friday and asked me to be there on Monday.

The proposal was due the following Monday, and I knew that it would be a difficult week but I was prepared for that. I had also explained to my client that I required a great deal of staff support to get any kind of proposal together in one week. He assured me that they had a great deal of material already collected and more coming in from others, firms that would be subcontractors.

I found the firm to be small indeed, with only one employee assigned to work with me full time, although he was most helpful and effective. As soon as I arrived, I had to start making plans, if they merit that term (the word *improvisations* is probably more accurate here). Even with working late every night, using several computers, and staying over an extra day it was a most difficult job, and its completion was made possible only by improvising changes in plans almost hourly to meet and overcome unexpected problems and disappointments.

The loss of 10 days while the client deliberated almost doomed the project. It is not unusual for clients to postpone decision making for one reason or another in this kind of situation. Obviously, those who do not have a great deal of direct experience in developing proposals are unmindful of the fact that there is rarely enough time in even the original proposal schedule, and losing time in getting started seriously compromises not only the quality of the proposal but also the probability of success in winning the contract. Therefore it is necessary to make swift decisions when the available time to carry out a project is short to begin with. Even more to the point, a great deal of help can be had by bringing on a consultant for a single day or a few hours to discuss the project, even if you must pay the consultant for that time. It will usually prove to be a good investment, for you get two benefits: First, you have the opportunity to evaluate the consultant and decide whether he or she is acceptable to you before you have committed more than a few hours. Second, if you have an acceptable consultant, you get the advantage of his or her recommendations and a head start on the project. It usually turns out to be cheap insurance.

Chapter Eleven

Evaluating the Results

Evaluation of results adds another dimension of benefits to the use of consultants.

WHY EVALUATE?

Management in your organization may require you to submit a formal report on the results of employing a consultant to help you. Or you might need such a report to justify and help you gain approval for future requests for consulting help. Or perhaps you use consultants frequently or with some regularity. In any of these cases you might find it helpful to establish a private directory to help you find and retain the best consultants when the need arises again. To develop such a list, you need to make a record of each consultant's areas of expertise and services and judge and record your evaluations of the consultant's performances in the various areas. The worksheet shown in Figure 11–1 suggests an approach to this.

The worksheet is deliberately designed for write-in entries, rather than check-offs, and ample space is provided for remarks, although the back of the form may also be used or sheets may be added. The worksheet also provides suggestions for remarks including the following.

Enthusiasm. Enthusiasm on the job is a positive trait, inspiring enthusiasm in others, and it also indicates the depth and degree of the consultant's interest in the task. It is worth noting as a desirable trait for most kinds of assignments.

Leadership. In many cases leadership ability is desirable. In my own consulting work I am often called upon to lead the client's staff in writing and assembling a proposal, for example, and that may be the case in many other kinds of assignments.

Presentation. This term has more than one application and meaning. On some occasions it refers to a formal presentation to an assembled group—a "dog-and-pony show," as many refer to it—but there are also occasions when it refers to instruction of your staff by the consultant, whether in formal groups or spontaneously while providing basic services.

Efficiency. Efficiency is an important factor in an individual

CONSULTANT PERFORMANCE EVALUATION

Consultant's name: ______________________________

Address: ______________________________

Telephone: ______________________________

Specialties: ______________________________

____

PERFORMANCE ON THE JOB

General: ______________________________

Technical skills: ______________________________

Communications skills: ______________________________

Writing ability: ______________________________

Presentations: ______________________________

Relationships with staff: ______________________________

Judgment: ______________________________

Cooperation: ______________________________

Dependability: ______________________________

Schedule adherence: ______________________________

Remarks and recommendations: ______________________________

____

____

____

Suggested entries:

Excellent Superior Good Fair Poor Satisfactory Unsatisfactory

Suggested other topics for comment:

Enthusiasm	Leadership	Presentation
Efficiency	Effectiveness	Openness

Figure 11–1. Worksheet to Evaluate Consultant's Performance.

who is costing you hundreds of dollars every day. Whereas you might usually permit a newly hired employee a couple of weeks, or even longer, to become oriented and begin to make a full contribution to your organization, you cannot afford that luxury with a consultant, not only from the dollar-cost viewpoint, but often from the schedule viewpoint. Quite often, clients call on consultants at the 11th hour, when it becomes obvious that some extra help is going to be needed to meet a goal. Thus it is urgent that the consultant be efficient enough to get aboard within hours and start becoming fully productive the first day of the assignment.

Effectiveness. Effectiveness is closely related to efficiency, and yet it is not the same thing, for effectiveness refers to the degree to which the desired end result is achieved. A consultant may be efficient—finish whatever work he or she does with great dispatch—and yet not produce the result desired. It can be important to your evaluation to make this distinction.

Openness. Openness is a subject that has arisen earlier in these pages. It refers to the consultant's willingness to share what he or she knows with you and your staff. It means that the honest and conscientious consultant does not hold back information and know-how that you, the client, have paid for and are entitled to. Openness means explaining *why*, as well as *what*, the consultant does or recommends doing.

Appendix

Frequently, directories and lists such as those offered here are the swiftest and most direct way of finding what you seek.

Appendix

REFERENCES AND STARTER LISTS

This book was designed to orient you to the world of consultants. It offered a number of ideas and items of information on how to seek out the consultants you need. In addition, there are many specific tools you will want to have readily available when the need for them arises. It is not necessary to commit any of them to memory: A number of lists are offered here as references to save you time in searching out consultants and applying some of the ideas offered in the pages that have gone before. This appendix is something of a potpourri, rather than being concentrated in any one area; it consists of data, information, and guidelines you are likely to need again and again in turning out proposal requests, sending out inquiries, evaluating proposals, or compiling bidders' lists, among other uses.

CATEGORIES OF CONSULTANTS

Some of the following terms are generic nouns and some are adjectives, but all have been taken from actual advertising and listings in directories and other sources. They reflect the images consultants have of themselves and the terms they use to identify themselves and describe their services and special fields. They are intended to be a help in determining what kinds of consultants are normally available and so to help you identify or define your own needs in relevant terms.

Administrative systems
Advertising
Airport management
Alcohol abuse
Apparel
Appraisers
Art
Auctioneers
Audio systems
Audiovisual presentations
Auditing
Automotive
Banking
Beauty

Categories of Consultants

Biofeedback
Bridal
Business development
Business writing
Career counseling
Catering
City government
Club management
Collection
Communications
Computer hardware
Computer programming
Computer software
Computer systems
Copy writers
Cosmetics
Cost benefit
Credit
Customs
Data communications
Data processing
Direct mail
Drug abuse
Economists
Editorial
Education
Energy
Engineering
Entertainment
Environmental analysis
Environmental control
Environmental hazards
Executive search
Export/import
Finance and accounting
Financial management
Fingerprint
Fire prevention
Food preparation
Foreign marketing
Forms design
Fund raising
Government contracting
Grants/grantsmanship
Graphics design
Health care
Health maintenance organizations
Hospital
Hotel management
Import/export
Industrial methods
Industrial psychology
Industrial relations
Insurance adjusters
Insurance advisors
Interior decorating
Investment
Labor relations
Legal
Lighting
Mail order
Mailing lists
Management
Market research
Marketing
Marriage
Meetings management
Mergers and acquisitions
Mergers and divestitures
Methods engineering
Municipal services
New product planning
Office design
Office methods
Office procedures
Organizational development
Packaging design
Pensions
Placement

Political campaigns
Printing
Product design
Product development
Product planning
Productivity
Profit control
Profit management
Profit sharing
Proposal writing
Psychology
Public relations
Publishing, general
Recreation
Sales
Sales promotions
Sales trainers
Security
Shipping
Technical publications
Telephone
Test methods
Training
Travel
Value engineering
Word processing

PERIODICALS

The periodicals listed here are among many that are useful aids in finding consultants. This list is merely exemplary and is by no means a complete list of all the newsletters, tabloids, and magazines that reach consultants and other professionals. However, there is an abundance of periodicals in every professional, business, and industrial field you can name. There are also sources for finding the names and addresses of such periodicals. Two such sources are the *Writer's Market*, an annual publication of the publisher of the monthly magazine, *Writer's Digest*, 1507 Dana Avenue, Cincinnati, OH 45207, and *The Newsletter Yearbook Directory*, published by The Newsletter Clearinghouse, 44 West Market Street, Rhinebeck, NY 12572.

Business Opportunities Digest 301 Plymouth Drive, NE Dalton, GA 30720	Monthly newsletter of business leads read by consultants, financial brokers, and others
Consultants News Templeton Road Fitzwilliam, NH 03447	Monthly newsletter addressed to consultants in general

Consulting Opportunities Journal P.O. Box 430 Clear Spring, MD 21722	Newsletter addressed to consultants in general
Direct Response Specialist P.O. Box 1075 Tarpon Springs, FL 34286	Monthly newsletter addressed to everyone in direct-response marketing
DM News 19 West 21st Street New York, NY 10010	Semimonthly tabloid covering the direct-response marketing field
In Business P.O. Box 323 Emmaus, PA 18049	Bimonthly magazine for small businesses and self-employed individuals
Meeting News 1515 Broadway New York, NY 10010	Monthly tabloid covering meetings and conventions, including their management
Meetings & Conventions 1 Park Avenue New York, NY 10016	Monthly magazine addressed to everyone concerned with the subject
Sharing Ideas! 18825 Hicrest Road Glendora, CA 91740	Bimonthly magazine addressed to professional speakers, writers, and consultants
Training 50 South 9th Street Minneapolis, MN 55402	Monthly slick-paper magazine addressed to professionals in training and consulting

PROFESSIONAL ASSOCIATIONS

Americans are joiners. There are thousands of associations of all kinds—trade associations, businesspeople's clubs, professional societies, and many others. For example, there are at least 35 consultants' associations. However, bear in mind that consulting is not a profession in itself; rather, it is a way many professionals, subprofessionals, and paraprofessionals choose to practice their professions. Therefore the rosters and membership lists of consultants' associations do not represent all consultants by any means. Many consultants choose to belong to one or another association, whether designated for consultants or not, and many choose not to belong to an association at all. Therefore, all of the listings here may be directly relevant to any quest you may have in the future for consulting help.

The following is only a beginning list of consulting, technical, and related associations. In most cases these are national or headquarters offices, but many of the organizations have local chapters in various cities, possibly in your own city. Use them as you see fit. The organization is alphabetical, by name, and has no significance other than that.

American Academy of Environmental Engineers
P.O. Box 269
Annapolis, MD 21404

American Association of Hospital Consultants
1235 Jefferson Davis Highway
Arlington, VA 22202

American Association of Medico-Legal Consultants
2200 Benjamin Franklin Parkway
Philadelphia, PA 19130

American Association of Political Consultants
444 North Capitol Street, NW
Washington, DC 20001

American Bankers Association
1120 Connecticut Avenue
Washington, DC 20036

American Consultants League
2030 North 16th Street
Arlington, VA 22201

American Consulting Engineers Council
1015 15th Street, NW
Washington, DC 20005

American Institute of Banking
1120 Connecticut Avenue, NW
Washington, DC 20036

American Institute of Certified Public Accountants
1211 Avenue of the Americas
New York, NY 10020

American Psychological Association
1200 17th Street, NW
Washington, DC 20036

Professional Associations

American Society for Hospital Risk Management
840 North Lake Shore Drive
Chicago, IL 60611

American Society for Industrial Security
1655 North Fort Myer Drive
Arlington, VA 22209

American Society for Information Science
1010 16th Street, NW
Washington, DC 20036

American Society of Agricultural Consultants
8301 Greensboro Drive
McLean, VA 22101

American Society of Appraisers
1180 Sunrise Valley Drive
Reston, VA 22091

American Society of Consultant Pharmacists
2300 9th Street South
Arlington, VA 22204

American Society of Consulting Arborists
315 Franklin Road
North Brunswick, NJ 08902

American Society of Consulting Planners
1717 N Street, NW
Washington, DC 20036

Armed Forces Communications and Electronics Association International
5641 Burke Center Parkway
Burke, VA 22015

Association for Supervision and Curriculum Development
225 North Washington Street
Alexandria, VA 22314

Association of Behavioral Trial Consultants
5201 North 7th Street
Phoenix, AZ 85014

Association of Bridal Consultants
29 Ferriss Estate
New Milford, CT 06776

Association of Consulting Chemists and Chemical Engineers
50 East 41st Street
New York, NY 10017

Association of Consulting Foresters
5410 Grosvenor Lane
Bethesda, MD 20814

Association of Executive Search Consultants
151 Railroad Avenue
Greenwich, CT 06830

Association of Federal Communications Consulting Engineers
P.O. Box 19333
1730 M Street, NW
Washington, DC 20036

Association of Graphic Arts Consultants
1730 North Lynn Street
Arlington, VA 22209

Appendix

Association of Internal Management Consultants
P.O. Box 155
Cranford, NJ 07016

Association of Management Analysts in State and Local Governments
P.O. Box 1027
Savannah, GA 31402

Association of Management Consultants
500 North Michigan Boulevard
Chicago, IL 60611

Association of Management Consulting Firms
230 Park Avenue
New York, NY 10169

Association of Masters of Business Administration Executives
305 Madison Avenue
New York, NY 10165

Association of Outplacement Consulting Firms
660 East 42nd Street
New York, NY 10165

Association of Productivity Specialists
200 Park Avenue
New York, NY 10166

Association of Professional Material Handling Consultants
1548 Tower Road
Winnetka, IL 60093

Association of Trial Behavior Consultants
5201 North 7th Street
Phoenix, AZ 85014

Automated Procedures for Engineering Consultants
Miami Valley Tower
Dayton, OH 45402

Direct Marketing Association
6 East 43rd Street
New York, NY 10017

Industrial Designers Society of America
6802 Poplar Place
McLean, VA 22101

Institute of Certified Professional Business Consultants
221 North LaSalle Street
Chicago, IL 60601

Institute of Management Consultants
19 West 44th Street
New York, NY 10036

Institute of Risk Management Consultants
58 Diablo View
Orinda, CA 94563

International Association of Book Publishing Consultants
485 Fifth Avenue
New York, NY 10017

International Association of Chiefs of Police
13 Firstfield Road
Gaithersburg, MD 20760

Professional Associations

International Association of Fire Chiefs
1329 18th Street, NW
Washington, DC 20036

International Association of Merger and Acquisition Consultants
11258 Goodnight
Dallas, TX 75229

International Association of Planning Consultants
P.O. Box 5198
Akron, OH 44313

International Association of Word Processing Specialists
1669 South Voss
Houston, TX 77057

International City Management Association
1120 G Street, NW
Washington, DC 20036

International College of Real Estate Consulting Professionals
1908 First Bank Place West
Minneapolis, MN 55402

International Communications Industries Association
3150 Spring Street
Fairfax, VA 22030

National Alliance of Independent Crop Consultants
Rt 1, Box 56K
Bishop, GA 30621

National Association for Community Development
1424 16th Street, NW
Washington, DC 20036

National Association of Air Traffic Specialists
415 Wheaton Plaza North
Wheaton, MD 20902

National Association of Business Economists
28349 Chagrin Boulevard
Cleveland, OH 44122

National Association of Credit Management
475 Park Avenue
New York, NY 10016

National Association of Energy Services
1133 15th Street, NW
Washington, DC 20005

National Association of Financial Consulting
10730 East Bethany Drive
Aurora, CO 80014

National Association of Freight Transportation Consultants
3436 Tanterra Circle
Brookville, MD 20833

National Association of Pension Consultants and Administrators
Three Piedmont Center
Atlanta, GA 30342

National Association of Vision Program Consultants
1775 Church Street, NW
Washington, DC 20036

National Association of Vision
Program Consultants
1775 Church Street, NW
Washington, DC 20036

National Beauty Culturists
League
25 Logan Circle, NW
Washington, DC 20005

National Business Education
Association
1914 Association Drive
Reston, VA 22091

National Council of Acoustical
Consultants
66 Morris Avenue
Springfield, NJ 07081

National Institute of Certified
Moving Consultants
124 South Royal Street
Alexandria, VA 22314

National Institute of
Governmental Purchasing
1735 Jefferson Davis Highway
Arlington, VA 22209

National Society of Professional
Engineers
2029 K Street, NW
Washington, DC 20006

National Speakers Association
4323 North 12th Street
Phoenix, AZ 85014

Professional Services Council
1825 Eye Street
Washington, DC 20006

Project Management Institute
P.O. Box 3
Drexel Hill, PA 19026

Society of Financial Examiners
P.O. Box 2598
Raleigh, NC 27602

Society of Professional Business
Consultants
221 North LaSalle Street
Chicago, IL 60601

Society of Professional
Management Consultants
P.O. Box 214
Sea Girt, NJ 08750

Washington Independent
Computer Consultants
Association
402 Maple Avenue West
Vienna, VA 22180

NETWORKS AND REFERRAL SERVICES

The following are consultant networks or referral services to which consultants subscribe. They are a source of assignments for consultants and a source of names for your bidders' lists.

Networks and Referral Services

Consultant Brokerage
P.O. Box 11485
Alexandria, VA 22312

Consultant Referral Service
P.O. Box 490175
Key Biscayne, FL 33149

Consultant Capacities Group, Inc.
3 Harbor Road
Cold Spring Harbor, NY 11724

Consultant Network
2120 Jimmy Durante Boulevard
Del Mar, CA 92014

CONSULTANT LABOR CONTRACTORS

The following are a few of the many firms in the United States that contract to supply engineers, technical writers, mathematicians, physicists, designers, packagers, computer systems analysts, and many other such technical and professional specialists as temporary labor, a rather specialized form of consulting. In many cases these firms are well known as suppliers of office temporaries, but they also have less well-publicized divisions (because of their more specialized applications) that supply technical/professional specialists as temporaries. Many of these firms maintain offices in numerous areas of the United States, wherever their major markets are, such as the New York, Boston, Philadelphia, Los Angeles, Dallas-Fort Worth, and Washington metropolitan areas. Regardless of the address listed here, you will find it worthwhile to look in your local telephone directory to see whether the firm has a local office or whether there are others in your area offering the service. (Actually, location does not matter too greatly, since the temporaries supplied by these contractors are generally individuals who will accept assignments almost anywhere.)

Augmentation, Inc.
8811 Colesville Road
Silver Spring, MD 20910

Consultants and Designers
355 Lexington Avenue
New York, NY 10017

Cummings Consultants, Inc.
P.O. Box 589
South Orange, NJ 07079

GP Technology Corporation
5615 Landover Road
Hyattsville, MD 20785

H. L. Yoh Company
210 West 230th Street
New York, NY 10034

JDG Associates, Ltd.
1700 Research Boulevard
Rockville, MD 20850

Kidde Consultants, Inc.
1020 Cromwell Bridge Road
Baltimore, MD 21204

Lion Head Technical
Consultants
275 Broadhollow Road
Melville, NY 11747

Mantech International Corp.
25 West Northfield Drive
Livingston, NJ 07039

Mantech Services Corporation
2121 Eisenhower Avenue
Alexandria, VA 22314

Manufacturing Consulting
Services, Inc.
3195A Airport Loop Drive
Costa Mesa, CA 92626

Miles-Samuelson, Inc.
15 East 26th Street
New York, NY 10010

Nayco Computer Systems
P.O. Box 2062
Columbia, SC 29202

Network Strategies, Inc.
8991 Cotswold Drive
Burke, VA 22015

Pinkerton Computer Consultants
5881 Leesburg Pike
Baileys Crossroads, VA 22041

Resource Consultants, Inc.
8200 Greensboro Drive
McLean, VA 22102

Staffing Consultants
8027 Leesburg Pike
Vienna, VA 22182

TAD Technical Corporation
P.O. Box 17012
Washington, DC 20041

TECH-ED Services
5020 Sunnyside Avenue
Beltsville, MD 20705

TECHPLAN Corporation
2001 Jefferson Davis Highway
Arlington, VA 22202

TECHSEARCH
11428 Rockville Pike
Rockville, MD 20852

Volt Information Sciences, Inc.
101 Park Avenue
New York, NY 10017

OUTLINE FOR WRITING RFPs AND EVALUATING PROPOSALS

Fairly extensive coverage was given to the subject of writing RFPs and evaluating proposals because proposals are an important tool for both the consultant and the client. Therefore, it seems useful to furnish an outline that can be used both for writing the RFP, with its statement of work, and for evaluating proposals submitted.

Elements of the RFP

1. Cover letter
    a. Summarize need/problem
    b. Announce that this is an RFP
    c. Identify party in your organization who will manage procurement, answer questions, otherwise manage and administer
    d. Give due date
    e. Announce any other special event, such as a preproposal meeting

2. Statement of work
    a. Describe need/problem as specifically as possible
    b. Describe surrounding or special conditions and/or constraints
    c. Specify desired end result, both quantitative and qualitative
    d. Specify interim and end products required—reports, tape, manuals, etc.
    e. Specify schedule(s)

f. Describe/specify any special conditions or requirements

3. Proposal requirement
   a. Specify information required
      (1) Evidence that consultant understands need/problem
      (2) Consultant's credentials—academic, experience, achievements
      (3) Other qualifications—resources and references
      (4) Specific approach proposed
      (5) Detailed plan, including lists of tasks and subtasks
      (6) Proposed schedule
      (7) Detailed specification of results and end products
   b. Discuss format
      (1) Suggest approximate format, but do not make it too restrictive
      (2) List items of information

SUGGESTED READINGS

Bell, Chip R., and Leonard Nadler. *The Client-Consultant Handbook*. Houston: Gulf, 1979.

Bermont, Hubert. *How to Become a Successful Consultant in Your Own Field*. Sarasota, FL: Consultant's Library, 1978.

Bermont, Hubert. *Principles and Practices of Professional Consulting*. Sarasota, FL: Consultant's Library, 1982.

Chaudier, Louann, ed. *Leading Consultants*. Highland Park, IL: J. Dick, 1984.

Fuchs, Jerome H. *Making the Most of Management Consulting Services*. New York: AMACOM, 1975.

Holtz, Herman. *How to Succeed as an Independent Consultant*. 2nd ed. New York: Wiley, 1988.

Holtz, Herman, and Terry Schmidt. *The Winning Proposal: How to Write It*. New York: McGraw-Hill, 1981.

Directories

Hunt, Alfred. *The Management Consultant.* New York: Wiley, 1977.

Lant, Jeffrey L. *The Consultant's Kit: Establishing and Operating Your Successful Consulting Business.* 2nd ed. Cambridge: JLA Publications, 1984.

Steele, Fritz. *The Role of the Internal Consultant.* Boston: CBI Publishing, 1982.

DIRECTORIES

Bradford's Directory of Marketing Research Agencies & Management Consultants. Bradford's, P.O. Box 276, Fairfax, VA 22030.

Consultants & Consulting Organizations Directory. Gale Research Co., Book Tower, Detroit, MI 48226.

Encyclopedia of Associations. Gale Research Co., Book Tower, Detroit, MI 48226.

National Trade & Professional Associations of the U.S. Columbia Books, Inc., 777 14th Street, NW, Washington, DC 20005.

Ulrich's International Periodicals Directory. R. R. Bowker Co., 1180 Avenue of the Americas, New York, NY 10036.

INDEX

A

B

C

F

Q

R

W

X